BLESSINGS & RITUALS

FOR THE JOURNEY OF LIFE

SUSAN LANGHAUSER

ABINGDON PRESS
Nashville

D1167031

BLESSINGS AND RITUALS FOR THE JOURNEY OF LIFE

Copyright © 2000 by Abingdon Press

Book design by J. S. Laughbaum

This book is printed on acid-free paper.

Library of Congress Cataloging-in-Publication Data

Langhauser, Susan, 1952–
    Blessings & rituals for the journey of life/Susan Langhauser.
    p. cm.
    Includes bibliographical references.
    ISBN 0-687-07437-1 (alk. paper)
    1. Benediction.   I. Title: Blessings and rituals for the journey of life. II. Title.

BV199.B4 L36 2000
264'.13—dc21   99-046789

00 01 02 03 04 05 06 07 08 09—10 9 8 7 6 5 4 3 2 1

MANUFACTURED IN THE UNITED STATES OF AMERICA

BLESSINGS AND RITUALS
FOR THE JOURNEY OF LIFE

To the people of Advent:
with deepest gratitude
for our shared ministry.

CONTENTS

CHAPTER THREE

Daily Living: Blessing
Rituals for Everyday Life   63

CHAPTER FOUR

Letting Go: Blessing Rituals
for Pastoral Care   92

CHAPTER FIVE

Creating Blessing Rituals 124

PREFACE

I have always been a person for whom rituals were important. Long before I realized that the church I attended was ritual based, I felt comfortable worshiping in a structured kind of atmosphere. When I left home for college and began my personal search for a church home (that age-old ritual which often includes dropping out for awhile), I discovered that churches that had no formal liturgical structure were places of interest, but not places where I could connect with God.

In my personal life I find routine comforting. In fact, I have described my own daily pattern of living as my "rut-tine," doing everyday tasks in a way that creates a foundation for my inner calm. My family will tell you that if those routines go unpracticed for too long, I am liable to be cranky and irritable, searching for some other way to make sense of my day, to "organize my chaos." Others might describe me as a control freak.

I have found myself ritualizing passages without thinking. Whether it was toasting with dear friends in empty rooms before walking out of my home in San Diego to go away to seminary or removing the necklace from an old boyfriend to formalize the end of our relationship (done in Hawaii, where it was given), I have always instinctively known that a symbolic action helps me move from one stage of life to the next more gracefully. Even if the passage leads me somewhere I have chosen and am excited about, these rituals are, for me, part of a necessary process of moving forward.

Thus far as a Lutheran pastor, I have found that many

people share this structuring process in their lives. Women seem to have a special gift for creating these symbolic gestures, often without even being aware that they are doing so. There exists, at least in my experience, a connection to the ordering of Creation that God initiated "in the beginning" that might cause us "created cocreators," both female and male, to exercise that same function in our own worlds.

Much has been written about the value of ritual for social living and the "why" of ritual effectiveness. I do not pretend to be a scholar on rituals, able to explore their history, their development, or the reasons why they work. All I know is that they do.

Recently, even best-sellers are addressing how rituals affect us, and how we might better serve our communities by establishing new rituals and reconnecting meanings to old ones for modern-day audiences, but few of these publications actually share any that have been used and are effective. The purpose of this book, then, is to provide actual rituals as a resource for those who need a place to begin. I hope that these rituals and blessings will be helpful in a variety of communities and settings and pave the road for clergy and laity to begin creating their own rituals in new and heretofore unritualized situations.

Some of these blessings are for formal liturgical church settings (although they can and should be easily adaptable to nonliturgical church use). Others may be used at home, during retreats, in the pastor's office, or in any setting predetermined by the people involved. Often ritual is most powerful in an untraditional location.

I invite you to use rituals and blessings. I commend my discoveries to you. Copy them, amend them, expand them, but *use* them to help your people connect to the power of God's Spirit in their daily lives. I have seen this process unburden souls, heal hurts, and energize for new adventures. I pray God uses them as such a vehicle for you and yours.

Some years ago there was an article by Neva Bryans in *Lectionary Homiletics* magazine that described a piece of sculpture called *Jesus Healing the Demoniac* by artist Tony Visco. The statue is of a young man leaning against Jesus, his back to Jesus' chest. Jesus is quieting him from behind, the boy's feet are completely off the ground, braced against Jesus' knees. His right hand is clutched in a fist flailing at the air over Jesus' head, while his head is thrown back against Jesus' breast. The left hand, however, is limp in surrender.

I think that this image is perfect for daily human living: we are all often in a state of unbalance, completely "off the ground" as it were. We fight the air with one hand while surrendering to the powers greater than we are with the other. The only thing that saves us is the strong arms of Jesus holding us up, embracing us close to his loving breast and allowing us to rest our weary heads on his shoulder. He is our rock, our support, our root in a world sometimes gone mad.

In a certain sense, I believe that ritual performs that same function for us. When the world or our own lives have become totally chaotic and out of control, we need to feel connected to something greater than ourselves, something unaffected by change and chaos. God's love for us and our rootedness in the promise of everlasting life and eternal caretaking is often the only constant in a constantly shifting world.

My family experienced the 1989 Loma Prieta earthquake, which shook the San Francisco Bay Area during the World Series. The morning after, although we were all safe and together, I had an overwhelming urge to leave the house and drive up the hill to Pacific Lutheran Theological Seminary, where my husband, Roger, and I were students. There, at chapel services, Dr. Timothy Lull preached a sermon based on Tillich's "Shaking of the Foundations." It was a powerful morning because of the preaching, but even more powerful for me was the connection to God in God's community of faith. It ordered the chaos, reminded me that we were not alone at the mercy of nature, and brought me back to a sense of structure and order that I would not have been able to attain on my own.

Rituals provide that kind of connection in a disconnected world. I commend the following pages to your use, with prayer, and with God's direction in your particular setting. May these rituals be a blessing in your ministry as they have been in mine, where they continue to enlighten, deepen, and strengthen my faith life and the connection of my faith community to the awesome fidelity of God.

At the Pacific Ocean
November 1998

ACKNOWLEDGMENTS

There are many people who have contributed to this little volume both with support for this project and with ideas and rituals of their own that I have used as a "springboard" for rituals included here. I am indebted to the Reverends Connie Winter-Eulberg and Steve Eulberg for the outline of the Blessing of a Baby in the Womb; for the Blessing of the Backpacks/Lunchboxes, colleagues the Reverend Julie Ebbesen and the Reverend Keith Hohly, who have used similar rituals originally envisioned by the Reverend Nancy Toensing.

The Reverend Rich Melheim has graciously given me his permission and blessing to "promote" the Faith Stepping Stones program and has encouraged me to share my work as widely as possible. Readers who are members of his Faith Inkubators Project will recognize the Faith Stepping Stone Blessings from the Faith Inkubators web site (www.faithink.com). Although these rituals are based on the Faith Stepping Stones framework provided by Pastor Melheim, I have written the actual rituals.

Many others have encouraged me to publish this book. I appreciate my local colleagues who have requested and used many of the works that follow. I also want to acknowledge the support and encouragement of Professor Martha Stortz of Pacific Lutheran Theological Seminary; Marianne Wilkinson, Executive Director of Hollis Renewal Center; and Carol E. Becker of Creative Communications, who continued to assist and provide counsel toward the realization of this book.

In addition, I want to thank my soul-friend Pastor Tim Johnson, who was there when many of these rituals were conceived and tried out for the first time. He has been an ongoing blessing to my life, and his friendship has been the bedrock of much that I have done.

Mom, Dad, and Laurie, I thank you for always loving me so well. And finally, thanks to my life-partner, my copastor, and my husband, Roger Gustafson, to whom I owe my capacity to love, my sometimes faltering maturity, and the continuing blessing that is our ministry together. Because of him, I am a "passable" stepmom to Andy and an all around better person. His love has given me the freedom and encouragement to move beyond my dreams and the security to use all the blessings God has provided. He is God's answer to my prayers.

INTRODUCTION

Blessings and rituals are a powerful way to connect God with people. Since I have begun using the blessings in this book, I have received numerous requests to provide copies or to create a ritual for a particular situation. Although the blessings that follow were originally written for use within a liturgical church setting, I am confident that it will be a simple task to adapt these for wider use in a variety of religious settings. Please feel free to use what works and change what does not for your particular and unique denomination or faith community.

I have made a number of assumptions that may or may not apply to your setting:

(1) These rituals and blessings are rooted in the promises God makes to us in Baptism and presuppose that Baptism is understood as a Sacrament, that is, "something God does for us, not something we do for God."

(2) Many of the rituals and blessings assume Baptism in the life of the participant. Should this not be the case in your situations, be aware of the need to edit, both practically and theologically.

(3) In chapter 4 especially, I am assuming the necessity for ordained clergy as leader in the cases where there is to be the administration of a Sacrament (Baptism, Communion, and in a lesser sense, Confession and Forgiveness) in connection with the ritual or blessing. If you are not ordained within your community of faith and have any hesitation about participating in these rituals without the authority of the pastoral office, please check with your

pastor or judicatory authority for the proper leadership and/or administration of any of the rituals offered here.

At the beginning of each chapter there is a brief introduction. For each ritual or blessing that follows there is a "Comments" section, which outlines what situation prompted the creation or adaptation of each ritual. This information should assist you in choosing the most appropriate ritual for your unique situations. In the pastoral care rituals, the comments have been culled from a variety of experiences. To ensure confidentiality, none is a complete example of a person or persons under my care. In some cases the examples are a compilation of a number of situations. In others the situations themselves have been altered.

Following the comments is a section marked "Items Needed," which denotes what props or elements you will need to prepare prior to beginning the ritual. This section, and all other instructions throughout the book, are designated by *italics* and will provide the step-by-step actions which may be used throughout each ritual or blessing.

The book is divided into four major chapters: Children, Adults, Everyday Life, and Pastoral Care. The first two are entitled "Stepping into . . ." and "Marking the Journey" and are so designated because they mark events or "passages" in the life of a Christian. Within these two chapters, a number of blessings are included called Faith Stepping Stones Blessings. These rituals were created to correspond with the Faith Stepping Stones program originally developed by Pastor Rich Melheim and the Faith Inkubators Project of Stillwater, Minnesota.

Faith Stepping Stones is a program that provides a structure in which to "bless the child, gift the family, and call parents back to the promises of Baptism" while affirming children as they take major steps along their faith journey's path. Our church has celebrated each Faith Stepping Stone with more than seven hundred children in the past three years, and we have seen a marked difference in the commitment level to the church community as a result. Our goal is to "knit them into the body of Christ" and make each child feel special with the laying on of hands, the giving of a blessing in church, and the presentation of a gift from the congregation to accompany each "step."

Originally the program was outlined in eight steps: (1) Baptism, (2) entry into Sunday school, (3) first Bible, (4) first Holy Communion, (5) entry into Confirmation, (6) the rite of Confirmation/entry into high school, (7) high school ministry, and (8) graduation from high school. In our church setting, we use only seven, so I have deleted the "step" for High School Ministry and used graduation from high school as Step #7.

Each Faith Stepping Stone includes a Family Class consisting of up to three meetings for the parents and participants. These meetings may include fellowship, education, and Bible study but are ongoing opportunities to gather a group of families who are experiencing each "passage" at the same time. This is a great way to begin some small group ministries, both because these are "safe" entry points into a congregation and because this group will experience each of their children's passages at the same time for years to come.

At the completion of each step's Family Classes, a Blessing in Church is held at least once every year. The Faith Stepping Stones Blessings which are included in the first two chapters are ones that I have written and are rooted in the promises made by parents and sponsors in the Sacrament of Holy Baptism as outlined in our *Lutheran Book of Worship*.

Finally, during the Blessing in Church, a gift from the congregation is given, appropriate to the passage and the age of the child. For more information about any aspect of the Faith Stepping Stones program, please contact Faith Inkubators at 1940 S. Greeley St., Suite 120, Stillwater, MN 55082, or visit their web site at www.faithink.com.

Chapters 3 and 4, "Daily Living" and "Letting Go," deal more with situations and experiences. It is my sincere hope that you will use this book to enhance your ministry and that you will continue to find ways to connect God and God's people in your ministry setting.

CHAPTER ONE

Stepping Into . . .

Blessing Rituals for Children

When I think of how a Christian community is to relate to its children, I would say that our responsibility is to love them, to teach them about God, and to provide an environment for them where they learn firsthand about right and wrong. However, when I think of Jesus and children, I am reminded by the Bible that Jesus spent most of his time simply "blessing" them. Following are a variety of blessings that can be conferred upon children. Some of them are for those special occasions that really are "faith stepping stones" and others are simply everyday moments that we can lift up to remind us and our little ones that God is a part of everything.

BLESSING OF A BABY IN THE WOMB

<u>Comments</u>: A young woman in my parish had just discovered that she was pregnant, and she was not really prepared for the news! She and her husband were both surprised, excited, and happy. But she spoke with me early on and revealed that she was a little resentful of the impending changes to her career, her family life, and her relationship with her spouse. At the same time, she was dealing with the recent deaths of two close friends, which only added to the normal fear and anxiety surrounding the new life growing inside her.

I had just read "Psalm During Pregnancy" by Edward Hays and had marveled at how a male could know so intimately the thoughts and fears of a woman carrying a child. It had embedded itself in my memory, and it seemed the perfect reading for this situation. At the same time, a clergy couple who were colleagues of ours were in the process of preparing for the birth of their son and had created an outline for this type of ritual. Many others have molded and shaped it as we have all sought to use it in our own ministry settings. Once performed, this ritual became very popular in our congregation, where there is a high incidence of births every year.

Note: Provide the names of your couple and of the child (if available) within this ritual.

Invocation

We begin in the name of the Father, and of the Son, and of the Holy Spirit. Amen.

Thanksgiving

Holy God, Mighty Lord, Gracious Creator: we give you thanks for the creation of the child of _____ and _____ , who is now being knit together by God within *(mother's)* body. This child is being held safe and secure in the waters of her womb, and for this water we give you thanks. We recall that in the beginning your Spirit moved over the waters and you created the heavens and the earth. By the gift of water, you nourish and sustain us and all living things.

Water gives us life and supports us. In the waters of Baptism we are given new life. We are cleansed by water. We live being nourished by water and we give you thanks for the gift of water and the gift of the new life you are creating now in the waters of *(mother's)* womb.

Psalm During Pregnancy—Edward Hays

I knew at once that something new had happened,
    a feeble, fleeting flutter of awareness.
I am now not I, but we; someone's deep within me,
    part of me but not me.
O Sacred Source of all, I am in awe at this new life
    within me,
    and I pray for the grace to carry it well,
    to honor the rhythms and seasons of the birthing cycle.
May I respect the morning sickness that comes to me
    even at sunset
    and the inner dance that keeps me awake
    through half-sleepless nights.
As I am sensitive to the changing contours of my body
    which are now beyond my ability to control—
    I wonder if my husband will still find me lovely—
    may I celebrate this season of change
    and the energy to provide for the needs

of this growing life within me
that these changes make possible.
Teach me the art of patient waiting,
    especially at those times when I wish
    that I could just take a peek inside
    to find out who this little person is
    who's tap dancing on my ribs while I try to sleep.
I want so much to be a good mother,
    to care for and nourish this new life.
Help me to gift this child with all the love I can,
    now during this time of pregnancy
    and also at each stage of life when I am called
    to set my baby free into fuller life.
O Holy Womb of Life, help me, for I am frightened;
    I do not feel ready for this awesome task.
Free me from my fear of a painful delivery;
    may it be a holy, harmonious experience for us both.
Free me from my fear of inadequacy
    about raising this child into maturity and holiness.
Please help me, Holy Parent,
    to protect my child who's yours as well;
    bring this baby safely through this birthing
    and the many other birthings in life.[1]

Prayer

O God, you are like a hen who gathers her chicks under
her wings. We pray that you would gather *(parents and
other children)* and this child under your wings as they go
through the process of birthing. As you sent your Son to
be born of Mary, we ask you to give _____ courage,
strength, and energy to do all that needs to be done in carrying and giving birth to this child. Calm her fears, provide release for her anxiety, and grant her the serenity to
behold with gracious wonderment this miracle she carries
within her.

We ask you to assist *(father)* in being a caregiver to
(mother), *(other children)*, and this child during this time of

pregnancy and birth. Give him energy, patience, understanding, and love for all his family.

We ask for understanding and love from *(other children)* that they may be good examples of loving children for their new brother or sister and aid their parents in the care of this child.

We pray that you would assist their extended family, their friends, and their doctors and nurses—all people offering care and support to this family. May you give them all the wisdom of your caring, healing, and strengthening Spirit.

These things, O God, we pray in the name of the One who called all children to come to him, our Lord and Savior Jesus Christ, and we now ask that you would bless this important time in the life of this family as we bless this child. Amen.

Individual Blessing and Laying on of Hands by the Pastor

BLESSING OF A BABY AT BIRTH

<u>Comments:</u> Since we have so many births in our congregation, I had been looking for a way to symbolize and announce the arrival of a child into our midst within our regular Sunday worship. Instead of the traditional rose on the altar, I had decided to place a small votive candle there for each birth. *(Since then I have purchased small glass holders in all the liturgical colors to match the paraments. Colored candles would work just as well.)*

Now, a story. A woman and her husband had lost a three-month-old baby girl shortly before we had arrived in the congregation. As a memorial, they had purchased a set of red paraments for the altar. Since their little girl's death, they had safely given birth to another girl and were expecting again. The morning their third child, a son, was born, I placed the votive candle on the altar. It was only as I entered in the processional that Pentecost morning that I realized their first child's red paraments were covering the altar, beneath the candle lit to welcome number three! This was a symbol for a big sister who would not be excluded from her family's happy day! The prayers that day were very special.

"For everything there is a season . . . a time to be born, and a time to die."—Ecclesiastes 3:1-2

WELCOMING A BABY INTO THE HOME/NEIGHBORHOOD

<u>Comments:</u> The idea of a "blessing/welcoming" box was described in great detail in the chapter entitled "Born" in Robert Fulghum's book *From Beginning to End: The Rituals of Our Lives.*[2] Although Fulghum includes words to perform the celebration, I have written a more formal ritual for his concept.

Items Needed: In preparation for this blessing ritual, all those who are invited must receive instructions regarding the ritual. Appoint a day and time and instruct them all to bring with them their contributions to be placed into a box, which will become a sort of "time capsule." Friends of the parents might bring snapshots of some favorite activity or event with a note explaining the rationale. Neighbors might include flyers from the latest block party or a significant neighborhood event that took place about the time of the child's birth. Family should certainly have no problem choosing some significant item which can be imbued with meaning as it is passed on to the child. Every effort should be made to include a note of explanation with each item—or at least videotape the gathering at the time of the filling of the box. (If video equipment is not available, enlist the help of a "recorder" who would write down the giver of each item and its significance. This avoids opening the box to exclamations of "And why did Bob Cratchit place a turkey bone in this box? Does anyone remember?!") Have a large box or basket prepared to receive items. This may be the box you actually use or just a temporary receptacle, depending on the quantity/size of gifts brought.

Leader: We begin in the name of the Father, and of the Son, and of the Holy Spirit. Amen.

Let us pray. Gracious Heavenly Father, you have given

this family/this community the gift of a brand new life. We gather today to celebrate this gift and to give you praise for the miracle that you have shared in our midst. Strengthen all of us to serve you by caring for this child as she/he grows. Make us all models of your love and compassion in our relationships with this child throughout the coming years; and at the end of all ages, bring us together at last into your glorious kingdom. We pray these things in Jesus' name. Amen.

At this time I invite each of you to share with this gathering the items you have brought for inclusion in _____'s Birth Box. Each gift reminds us of the gift God has given to us in this new life, as well as the gift of God's son, Jesus, so many years ago. We all share in the joy of this birth and have selected various things to share with ____ today.

(The participants now put the items in the Birth Box.)

Now that we have gathered and shared our stories, it is time to welcome this child. Please extend the right hand of blessing and join with me in the Aaronic Benediction (Num. 6:24-26):

> The LORD bless you and keep you;
> The LORD make his face to shine upon you and
>   be gracious to you;
> The LORD lift up his countenance upon you,
> And give you peace. Amen.

Notes: *Make sure to place a list of those who attended inside the Birth Box, which may be opened on a significant birthday. Ages 16 and 21 are appropriate, although for other reasons it may be decided to do so at another time. In the event that you still reside in the neighborhood where the welcoming took place, invitations might be sent to all those who originally attended. Obviously, if video recordings were made, a trip down a visual memory lane could ensue. Enjoy the party!*

ANNUAL BLESSING FOR CHILDREN BAPTIZED
FAITH STEPPING STONE #1
CHURCH BLESSING FOR "STEPPING INTO LIFE"

Comments: Our church was looking for a way to incorporate our children's faith journey into our worship life more effectively when we discovered the Faith Inkubator Project's Faith Stepping Stones program. Since the sacrament of Holy Baptism is regularly celebrated during our worship services, we wanted to find a way to acknowledge all of the children who had been baptized in the previous year at one time and take one more opportunity for baptismal conversation with parents who had already experienced it. The day we chose is the Baptism of Our Lord Sunday in January, although any baptismal festival day can be used. The baptismal promises cited in all seven of the Faith Stepping Stones Blessings are from the rite for Holy Baptism in the *Lutheran Book of Worship*. The ritual follows:

Leader: Today we take the first step in our Faith Stepping Stones program. Will the parents of the *children who have been baptized this past year* please stand.

In Christian love you presented these children for Holy Baptism. In Baptism, sacred promises are made. As parents of these children, it is your calling to keep these sacred promises:

- to faithfully bring them to the services of God's house
- to teach them the Lord's Prayer, the Creed, and the Ten Commandments
- to place in their hands the Holy Scriptures
- and to provide for their instruction in the Christian faith.[3]

Do you renew your commitment to these baptismal promises? If so, answer, **"I do, and I ask God to help and guide me."**

Leader: Congregation, do you promise to support and encourage these parents in the keeping of these sacred promises? If so, answer, **"We will, with God's help."**

Leader: One of the ways we begin knitting our children into the body of Christ is by bringing them into the community to be baptized and claimed by God as God's own. You have participated in this sacrament, and we celebrate today with you the new life you have provided for these children as born-again Christians, connected to this community of Christ.

(Further explanation of the preparation for this Stepping Stone may be added here. For example, "These families have met for the past month to talk about how to share their faith with their children, and they have committed to pray with and for their children as they begin their faith journey.")

Prayers

Leader: On this important day, when we celebrate the sacrament of Holy Baptism, we ask God's blessing on these newly baptized and the whole people of God in Christ Jesus. Let us pray: *(The Leader prays with standard or extemporaneous prayers. Each prayer may end:)*

Leader: Lord, in your mercy . . .
All: Hear our prayer.

(Prayers conclude with the Leader saying these or similar words:)
Into your hands, O Lord, we commend all for whom we

pray; trusting in your mercy, through your Son, Jesus Christ our Lord. Amen.

Leader: We invite all those who are participating in this Faith Stepping Stone to come forward one family at a time for the laying on of hands and to receive God's blessing and a gift from the congregation.

(If older children or adults were baptized, invite them to kneel. Lay on hands.)

Leader: _____ , I bless you in the name of Jesus Christ, our Lord.

(The gifts are given and the participants are seated. The rite may conclude with the sharing of the peace or other appropriate instruction.)

Leader: The peace of the Lord be with you always.
All: And also with you.

Suggestions for gifts: Baptismal medallions, baptismal shells, small baptismal-theme wall hanging, Christian children's music on tape/CD, lullabies on tape/CD, baptismal candles (if not given in the actual baptismal rite).

Blessing for Children
Entering Sunday School
(Approximately Age Three)
Faith Stepping Stone #2
Church Blessing for "Stepping into Sunday School"

Leader: Today we take another step in our Faith Stepping Stones program. Will the parents of those *three-year olds who have just begun attending Sunday school* please stand.

In Christian love you presented these children for Holy Baptism. In Baptism, sacred promises are made. As parents of these children, it is your calling to keep these sacred promises:

- to faithfully bring them to the services of God's house
- to teach them the Lord's Prayer, the Creed, and the Ten Commandments
- to place in their hands the Holy Scriptures
- and to provide for their instruction in the Christian faith.[4]

Do you renew your commitment to these baptismal promises? If so, answer, **"I do, and I ask God to help and guide me."**

Leader: Congregation, do you promise to support and encourage these parents in the keeping of these sacred promises? If so, answer, **"We will, with God's help."**

Leader: One of the ways we help you keep your promise is our Sunday school program. Sunday school is an important step in the life of a Christian because it is here that they are taught the Lord's Prayer, the Creed, and the Ten Commandments. Sunday school teaches them the great stories of our faith and begins the process of knitting them into the body of Christ on earth, the Church.

(Further explanation of this Stepping Stone may be added here.)

Prayers

Leader: On this important day, the day that you "Step into Sunday school," we ask God's blessing on you and the whole people of God in Christ Jesus. Let us pray: *(The Leader prays either standard or extemporaneous prayers. Each prayer petition may end:)*

Leader: Lord, in your mercy . . .
All: Hear our prayer.

(Prayers conclude with:)
Leader: Into your hands, O Lord, we commend all for whom we pray; trusting in your mercy, through your Son, Jesus Christ our Lord. Amen.

Leader: We invite those who have completed the Family Class for Stepping into Sunday School to come forward for the laying on of hands, and to receive God's blessing and a gift from the congregation.

(Each child is invited to kneel for the laying on of hands.)
Leader: _____ , I bless you in the name of Jesus Christ, our Lord.

(The gifts are given and the participants are seated.)

Leader: The peace of the Lord be with you always.
All: And also with you.

Blessing for Receiving First Bibles
(Approximately Spring of Second Grade)
Faith Stepping Stone #3
Church Blessing for "Stepping into the Word"

Comments: The Family Class for this step is three nights in which parents and children highlight verses from every book in the Bible. At the conclusion, parents write a special message inside the front cover for their child. Here's the ritual:

Leader: Today we take another step in our Faith Stepping Stones program. Will the parents of the children *receiving their Bibles* please stand.

In Christian love you presented these children for Holy Baptism. In Baptism, sacred promises are made. As parents of these children, it is your calling to keep these sacred promises:

- to faithfully bring them to the services of God's house
- to teach them the Lord's Prayer, the Creed, and the Ten Commandments
- to place in their hands the Holy Scriptures
- and to provide for their instruction in the Christian faith.[5]

Do you renew your commitment to these baptismal promises? If so, answer, **"I do, and I ask God to help and guide me."**

Leader: Congregation, do you promise to support and encourage these parents in the keeping of these sacred promises? If so, answer, **"We will, with God's help."**

Leader: One of the ways we keep the promise "to place in their hands the Holy Scriptures" is to give you and your child a Bible for devotions and family prayer. This is an important step in the life of Christians, and we celebrate with you today this Faith Stepping Stone.
(Further explanation of preparation for this Stepping Stone may be added here.)

Prayers

Leader: *(Stand)* On this important day, the day that many of our children step into the Word, we ask God's blessing on them and on the whole people of God in Christ Jesus. Let us pray:

(All petitions may end with :)
Leader: Lord, in your mercy . . .
All: Hear our prayer.

(Prayers may conclude with:)
Leader: Into your hands, O Lord, we commend ourselves and all for whom we pray; trusting in your mercy, through your Son, Jesus Christ our Lord. Amen. *(Sit)*

Leader: All those who have completed the Family Class for Stepping into the Word are invited to come forward for the laying on of hands and God's blessing. Parents, please bring the Bibles you prepared in family class with you.

(The child is invited to kneel for the laying on of hands.)
Leader: _____ , I bless you in the name of Jesus Christ, our Lord.

Leader: We ask now that you as parents fulfill the promise that was made at Baptism. Place into your child's hands the Holy Scripture with the words **"Today I fulfill the promise."**

Parents: Today, I fulfill the promise. *(Bibles are given.)*

Leader: The peace of the Lord be with you always.
All: And also with you.

BLESSING FOR FIRST COMMUNICANTS
(Second Through Fourth Grade)
FAITH STEPPING STONE #4
CHURCH BLESSING FOR "STEPPING INTO FORGIVENESS"

Leader: Today we take another step in our Faith Stepping Stones program. Will the parents of the children *who are receiving their first Communion* please stand?

In Christian love you presented these children for Holy Baptism. In Baptism, sacred promises are made. As parents of these children, it is your calling to keep these sacred promises:

- to faithfully bring them to the services of God's house
- to teach them the Lord's Prayer, the Creed, and the Ten Commandments
- to place in their hands the Holy Scriptures
- and to provide for their instruction in the Christian faith.[6]

Do you renew your commitment to these baptismal promises? If so, answer, **"I do, and I ask God to help and guide me."**

Leader: Congregation, do you promise to support and encourage these parents in the keeping of these sacred promises? If so, answer, **"We will, with God's help."**

Leader: One of the ways we help you keep these promises and "provide for their instruction in the Christian faith" is to prepare them for their participation in the Lord's Supper. This is an important step in the life of a Christian because it is here that we receive God's forgiveness and are strengthened for service by God's abiding love. This sacrament is a gift of God's love to you and your children. Today we celebrate with you this Faith Stepping Stone, "Stepping into Forgiveness."

(Further explanation of this particular Stepping Stone may be added here.)

Prayers

Leader: On this important day, the day that you step into forgiveness by receiving your first Holy Communion, we ask God's blessing on you and the whole people of God in Christ Jesus. Let us pray:

(Petitions may end with :)
Leader: Lord, in your mercy . . .
All: Hear our prayer.

(Prayers may conclude :)
Leader: Into your hands, O Lord, we commend ourselves and all for whom we pray; trusting in your mercy, through your Son, Jesus Christ our Lord. Amen.

Leader: At this time we invite all those who have completed the Family Class for Stepping into Forgiveness to come forward for the laying on of hands, and to receive God's blessing and a gift from the congregation.

(Each child is invited to kneel for the laying on of hands.)
Leader: _____ , I bless you in the name of Jesus Christ, our Lord.

(The gifts are given, and the participants are seated. The rite may be concluded:)
Leader: The peace of the Lord be with you always.
All: And also with you.

BLESSING FOR ENTERING CONFIRMATION
(Sixth or Seventh Grade)
FAITH STEPPING STONE #5
CHURCH BLESSING FOR "STEPPING INTO THE CHURCH"

Leader: Today we take another step in our Faith Stepping Stones program. Will the parents of the young people *entering Confirmation* please stand.

In Christian love you presented these children for Holy Baptism. In Baptism, sacred promises are made. As parents of these children, it is your calling to keep these sacred promises:

- to faithfully bring them to the services of God's house
- to teach them the Lord's Prayer, the Creed, and the Ten Commandments
- to place in their hands the Holy Scriptures
- and to provide for their instruction in the Christian faith.[7]

Do you renew your commitment to these baptismal promises? If so, answer, **"I do, and I ask God to help and guide me."**

Leader: Congregation, do you promise to support and encourage these parents in the keeping of these sacred promises? If so, answer, **"We will, with God's help."**

Leader: One of the ways we provide for their instruction in the Christian faith is the program of Confirmation. Entry into Confirmation is an important step in the life of the Christian. On the day of their Confirmation, these young adults will respond publicly to their Baptism, when God claimed them and made them part of the Church, the body of Christ on earth.

(Further explanation of this Stepping Stone may be added here.)

Prayers

Leader: On this important day, the day that you step into Confirmation, we ask God's blessing on you and the whole people of God in Christ Jesus.

Let us pray: Dear God of creation, we ask your blessing on these young people as they enter a new period in their lives of faith. Bless them and grant them your gifts: joy as they live among your faithful people; openness in hearing your Word and thankfulness in sharing your supper; eagerness in sharing the good news of Christ through their words and actions; dedication in serving all people following the example of the Lord Jesus; and a hunger for justice and peace.

(Other petitions may be included and may end with:)
Leader: Lord, in your mercy . . .
All: Hear our prayer.

(Prayers conclude with:)
Leader: Into your hands, O Lord, we commend ourselves and all for whom we pray; trusting in your mercy, through your Son, Jesus Christ our Lord. Amen.

Leader: All who are participating in this Faith Stepping Stone are invited to come forward for the laying on of hands, and to receive God's blessing and a gift from the congregation.

(Each young person may be invited to kneel for the laying on of hands.)
Leader: _____ , I bless you in the name of Jesus Christ, our Lord.

(The gifts are given and the participants are seated.)

Leader: The peace of the Lord be with you always.
All: And also with you.

CHAPTER TWO

Marking the Journey

Blessing Rituals for Adults

The following blessing rituals for "marking the journey" are significant because they mark an event or a passage and point to a future reality. Although volumes covering the details of marking passages already exist, few actually include a written ritual. All of the following rituals (excluding those that belong to the Faith Stepping Stones cycle) include an opportunity for the person ritualizing to identify a symbol that will be used during the rite.

Symbols, sometimes referred to as "earthly elements," can be viewed theologically as the means by which God comes to us. Seen within this context, all rituals have a measure of sacramental aspect to them, which may be, in fact, the reason rituals work to assist in the transformation process. This is discussed further in chapter 4.

Blessing for the Rite of Confirmation
(Approximately Ninth Grade)

Faith Stepping Stone # 6

Church Blessing for "Stepping into the Community"

Comments: Since most denominations have their own ritual for Confirmation I have not included that particular rite. However, our community of faith celebrates an additional Faith Stepping Stones blessing for those who have undergone the Rite of Confirmation, either within the Confirmation Rite itself or the next week.

Leader: Today we celebrate those who are taking another step in their faith journey through our Faith Stepping Stones program. Will the parents and sponsors of *the young people who have just been confirmed* please stand.

In Christian love you presented your children for Holy Baptism. In their Baptisms, sacred promises were made. As parents of these young *women/men,* it was part of your calling to see that those sacred promises were kept:

- to faithfully bring them to the services of God's house
- to teach them the Lord's Prayer, the Creed, and the Ten Commandments
- to place in their hands the Holy Scriptures
- and to provide for their instruction in the Christian faith.[1]

You have fulfilled those promises. We now ask you to renew the covenant you made within this congregation for the ongoing support of these young people's faith journeys. Do you intend to continue to worship, study, and pray regularly with your children? If so, answer, **"I do, and I ask God to help and guide me."**

Leader: Congregation, do you promise to support and encourage these parents and sponsors in the keeping of these sacred promises? If so, answer, **"We will, with God's help."**

Leader: *(To Confirmands)* You have been received into this fellowship *(if appropriate, add: as full voting members of this congregation).* This is a passage into adulthood unlike others you will experience, for it is surrounded by the Body of Christ as expressed in the community of this congregation. Do you intend to continue in the covenant you made within this community for the nurture of your own faith journeys, to continue to worship, study, and pray regularly? If so, answer, **"I do, and I ask God to help and guide me."**
(Further explanation of this Stepping Stone may be added here.)

Prayers

Leader: On this important day, the day when we mark your "Stepping into Community," we ask God's blessing on you and on the whole people of God in Christ Jesus.

Let us pray: Dear God of creation, we ask your blessing on these young people as they enter a new period in their lives of faith. Bless them and grant them your gifts: *joy* as they live among your faithful people; *openness* in hearing your Word and *thankfulness* in sharing your supper; *eagerness* in sharing the good news of Christ through their words and actions; *dedication* in serving all people following the example of the Lord Jesus; and a *hunger* for justice and peace.

(This and any other petitions may end:)
Leader: Lord in your mercy . . .
All: Hear our prayer.

(Prayers conclude)
Leader: Into your hands, O Lord, we commend all for whom we pray; trusting in your mercy, through your Son, Jesus Christ our Lord. Amen.

(If this ritual is done at a different time than the Rite of Confirmation, you may use the following:)
Leader: At this time we invite all those who are participating in this Faith Stepping Stone to come forward for the laying on of hands, and to receive God's blessing and a gift from the congregation.

(Each young person may be invited to kneel for the laying on of hands.)
Leader: _____ , I bless you in the name of Jesus Christ, our Lord.

(The gifts are given and the participants are seated. The peace may be shared.)
Leader: The peace of the Lord be with you always.
All: And also with you.

BLESSING FOR THOSE RECEIVING THEIR DRIVER'S LICENSES

Comments: This year in our community hundreds of young men and women completed an intensive driver's education program that prepares them to secure their "restricted" license at age 15. This allows them to drive to/from work or school only, and is given with an eye exam and certificate of completion of the driver's education program. As a parent, I felt the need to address the excitement of the students as well as the fears of the parents within the worship context.

Items Needed: Prior to this ritual, the young people should be asked to choose a symbol from their youth to bring to church. These could range from a Barbie doll to Star Wars books and will be given to the community. Each choice should be affirmed.

Leader: We begin in the name of the Father, and of the Son, and of the Holy Spirit. Amen.

We have gathered today to bless these young people as they step into new responsibilities and leave their younger years behind. Among ancient peoples, the rite of passage into adulthood has always been a quest connected to a more adult understanding of the world. These passages have been made with great effort of soul and with pride as well as the misgivings of their parents. Today we celebrate your new life as adult members of this community, marked with the permission of the state to operate a motor vehicle. Will those who have just received their driver's licenses please come forward?

(The young people come forward bringing their symbols. Each is invited to explain why their "symbol" was chosen.)

You have brought back to this community the trappings of your youth. We offer them to the larger community to be enjoyed by others as they continue on their journeys of life and faith. For you, they are symbols of time gone by, of a time that will never come again. There is some sadness in leaving the safety of this period in your lives, but at the same time, there is excitement at the new life about to be entered. *(The leader takes the driver's licenses.)* These are the symbols of your newly claimed adulthood. Carry them with humility and pride, but carry them with the acknowledgment that they are merely pieces of paper that give you the right to a new freedom.

We pray that in accepting this new freedom, you will also accept the God-given responsibilities of maturity. Use them as the means and opportunity to be people of God in a world that needs to know compassion and care.

As you fasten your seatbelt, ask for God's protection. Remember that you are precious in God's sight, and that you reflect God's world in the way you handle this new responsibility.

(The young people are invited to kneel for the laying on of hands.)
Leader: We bless you in the name of Jesus Christ, our Lord; and we ask God's Holy Spirit to accompany you on all your journeys, short or long, until that day when we rejoice together in the kingdom of heaven. Amen.

BLESSING FOR THOSE GRADUATING FROM HIGH SCHOOL

FAITH STEPPING STONE # 7

CHURCH BLESSING FOR "STEPPING INTO THE WORLD"

Leader: Today we celebrate those who are taking another step in their faith journey through our Faith Stepping Stones program. Will the parents of the *young people who are graduating from high school* please stand.

In Christian love you presented your children for Holy Baptism. In their Baptisms, sacred promises were made. As parents of these young women and men, it was part of your calling to see that those sacred promises were kept:

- to faithfully bring them to the services of God's house
- to teach them the Lord's Prayer, the Creed, and the Ten Commandments
- to place in their hands the Holy Scriptures
- and to provide for their instruction in the Christian faith.[2]

You have fulfilled those promises. We now ask you to covenant with this congregation for the ongoing support of these young people in their faith journeys. Do you intend to routinely lift your children up in prayer? If so, answer, **"I do, and I ask God to help and guide me."**

Leader: Congregation, do you promise to support and encourage these parents in the keeping of these sacred promises? If so, answer, **"We will, with God's help."**

Leader: *(To Graduates)* You have completed this congregation's Faith Stepping Stones program. Do you intend to continue in the covenant God made with you in Holy Baptism:

- to live among God's faithful people
- to hear God's Word and share in his supper
- to proclaim the good news of God in Christ through word and deed
- to serve all people, following the example of our Lord Jesus
- and to strive for justice and peace in all the earth?[3]

If so, answer, **"I do, and I ask God to help and guide me."** *(Further explanation of this Stepping Stone may be added here.)*

Prayers

Leader: On this important day, the day when we mark your "Stepping into the World," we ask God's blessing on you and on the whole people of God in Christ Jesus.

Let us pray: Dear God of creation, we ask your blessing on these young people as they enter a new period in their lives of faith. Bless them and grant them your gifts: *joy* as they live among your faithful people; *openness* in hearing your Word and *thankfulness* in sharing your Supper; *eagerness* in sharing the good news of Christ through their words and actions; *dedication* in serving all people following the example of the Lord Jesus; and a *hunger* for justice and peace.

(All petitions may end:)
Leader: Lord in your mercy . . .
All: Hear our prayer.

(Prayers conclude with:)
Leader: Into your hands, O Lord, we commend all for whom we pray; trusting in your mercy, through your Son, Jesus Christ our Lord. Amen.

Leader: We invite all those who completed the Faith Stepping Stones Family Class to come forward for the laying on of hands and to receive God's blessing and a gift from the congregation.

(The graduates are invited to kneel for the laying on of hands.)
Leader: _____ , I bless you in the name of Jesus Christ our Lord.

(The gifts are given and the participants are seated as the peace is shared.)
Leader: The peace of the Lord be with you always.
All: And also with you.

PREMARITAL OR WEDDING REHEARSAL BLESSING

Items Needed: The rings, license, unity candles, and paraphernalia that will be used in the wedding are brought to the altar by the couple prior to the ritual. If anointing will be done, be sure to have oil available.

Leader: We begin in the name of the Father, and of the Son, and of the Holy Spirit. Amen.

We have come into the house of the Lord to ask God's blessing on the trappings of the wedding to come. We know that God has used earthly things to convey God's presence for centuries, and we ask today that God will continue to richly bless the union of these two families in the persons of _____ and _____.

Always remember that you have been claimed by Christ in the waters of your baptisms, and that by joining together in God's presence, you are honoring God's plan for human love.

These **candles** symbolize the love of your families and their acknowledgment that now you will leave these families to create a new family together. You remain in their prayers and in their hearts, but you are released to find your own way together.

This **license** reminds you that you are at liberty to grow up together, but within the boundaries of a government of this world, submitting to its laws and statutes. It is not a bill of sale, but a "building permit" for you to use as you build your life together.

These **rings** symbolize the never ending care that God has taught us and that God desires for your life together. May you look upon them as binding and freeing: binding you to each other, and yet freeing you to become new creations within the loving context of the life you will be building together.

(With the laying on of hands or an anointing if desired.)
     _____ , I bless you in the name of Jesus Christ.
     _____ , I bless you in the name of Jesus Christ.
May you always remember that your first love is the love you receive from God in Jesus. Blessings on your new life, your new journey together. May it always be pleasing to the God who first gave you life. We pray in Jesus' name. Amen.

Note: *I have also used a "ring blessing" that was done by class-mates of mine at their wedding in Berkeley, California, while I was in seminary there. With an intimate gathering of friends, they passed the rings around for each of us to touch and place our own prayers for the couple and blessings upon. They then exchanged these rings that had become symbols not only of their love for one another, but of the love of their communities for them. If the congregation has fewer than one hundred people, I have passed through the assembling crowd prior to the ceremony, inviting the attendees to bless the couple's rings. It is sometimes a surprise to the couple, but one that has always been gratefully received, in a way, my gift to their marriage.*

BLESSING FOR A NEW HOUSE

<u>Comments:</u> Many house blessings are available in Occasional Services books. However, I believe this one would be especially meaningful to those having purchased their first new home, especially because they have an investment not only in the home, but in the ritual itself.

—⟨✦✦✦⟩—

Items Needed: To prepare, the family should be instructed to gather together items from each room of the house that symbolize the function of that space. Children should be encouraged to participate in choosing these items, for they see with different eyes. Each room may be symbolized by items chosen from as many family members as wish to participate. The leader should bring a light from the church, and if possible, the flame is taken from the Christ candle, as was the practice of ancient villagers, who each year lit their hearth fire from the "new fire" struck at the Easter Vigil. This candle is carried into each room, bringing the light of Christ into all the dwelling spaces. Finally, the candle's light is transferred to the family's candle in a location that they have chosen as central to or symbolic of their unique family situation. Assemble in that room all the family's symbols and make this room's blessing the one saved for last.

Leader: As Christ's light scatters the darkness in our lives, it comes into this home to bless those who will dwell herein.

(In the entry/foyer) Blessings on this dwelling place and all those who will go out and come in through this entryway.

(In the living room) Blessings on the guests who come to call and the family who gather here for celebrations great and celebrations small.

(In the dining room) Blessings on the table where meals are taken and time is shared. May this family always find the space in each day to sit together at table, for it is here our Lord's ministry was at its most powerful.

(In the study) Blessings on the work that is done in this home. "May the words of our lips and the meditations of our hearts be acceptable in your sight, O Lord."

(In the bedrooms) Blessings on these places of rest and refreshment. May we always be connected to God in our lying down and in our rising up.

(In the children's bedrooms) Blessings on the place of sanctuary for our little ones. May this space be full of care and creativity, prayer and time to be connected to God.

(In the family room) Blessings on this place of togetherness. May it always be filled with warmth and fellowship, with peace and the delight of time with each other.

(In the kitchen) Blessings on the food that is here and all the hands that will prepare it. May it nourish this family in body and spirit, for the work of Jesus Christ in the world.

(In the yard/on the deck, patio, or porch) Blessings on the activities that will center in this space created by God. May you always find delight in the Creation and your places in it.

(At the final location, where all symbols are assembled.)
Leader: Blessings on this family, on this house, and on all these symbols that signify this family's dwelling place.

(Read Deut. 6:4-9.)

Leader: Amen.

BLESSING FOR PERSONS WHO HAVE BEEN DIVORCED

<u>Comments:</u> Divorce is usually "crazy time." One day divorced persons may awaken feeling that they will be okay and that they are healing and will be able to go on, while the very next day they feel hopeless and terrible. To acknowledge that a divorce is just the beginning of an emotional roller coaster is to move beyond the popular idea that finalizing a relationship through the act of divorce somehow enables a person to magically pick up the pieces of his or her life and move on without significant reaction to the change. Obviously there are as many reasons for divorce as there are couples. Suffice it to say, those who seek pastoral counsel following a divorce probably had an initial sense of covenant/commitment that has been broken, and a deep sense of guilt about the failure of their marriage. Because they have come to the church to help mark this passage in their lives, the church must make every effort to assist in this marking in a theological context. Since this ritual contains elements of confession and forgiveness, pastoral leadership is recommended.

Items Needed: *Anything that symbolizes the coexistence of bitter and sweet can work here. Because my congregation routinely celebrates a Passover seder meal and is familiar with it, the charoset and horseradish combination has meaning, as well as placing this ritual in a framework reminiscent of the Holy Week paradox: Good Friday and Easter. A "marriage symbol," chosen by the participant(s) and oil for anointing if you so choose, should be close at hand, perhaps upon the altar or baptismal font.*

Leader: _____ *(and* _____ *if both persons are present),* you have come to God's house today to mark the passing of a dream, the vision of a marriage entered into with high hopes and sincere commitment.

(A symbol of the marriage may be placed upon the altar. In the case of a communal rite, the person may wish to explain the symbol and why it was chosen.)

In our marriage rite, we are reminded that "because of sin, our age-old rebellion, the gladness of marriage can be overcast and the gift of the family can become a burden."[4] It is with sadness that we acknowledge that your union, now ended, did not survive the pressures placed upon it, and it has been dissolved.

Leader: I ask you now to confess your part in the breaking down of the commitment:

Do you accept your measure of responsibility for the failure of this union? If so, answer, **"I do so confess."**

Do you promise to commend all of your emotions to God: the anger and the pain, the resentment and the grief, the confusion and the hurt, so that they can hold no power over you? If so, answer, **"I do so promise."**

Will you continue to pray for and to respect your former spouse, trusting in and claiming for yourself the spirit of reconciliation within the Body of Christ? If so, answer, **"I will, with the help of God."**

God continues to show mercy especially to those who feel the least worthy of such love. God has shown us through the death and resurrection of Jesus that our sins need not bind us. God has promised to provide the Holy Spirit to strengthen us in our repentance and to guide us in the paths of new life and growth. *"So if anyone is in Christ, there is a new creation: everything old has passed away; see, everything has become new!"* (2 Cor. 5:17).

As a called and ordained minister of the church of Christ, and by God's authority, I declare to you that you are forgiven. John's Gospel reminds us that *"unless a grain of wheat falls into the earth and dies, it remains just a single grain; but if it dies, it bears much fruit"* (John 12:24). You have experienced a sort of death, but upon that death a new life begins. In acknowledgment of the pain and the joy of this new beginning, eat this matzo spread with the bitter herbs of suffering and the sweetness of charoset.

(The marriage symbol may be brought forward and imbued with a new significance. This can be done either by the person or by the pastor in consultation with the person. For example, a wedding ring may be sold for a special purpose or ministry, saved and given to a child on coming of age, or used in some other "nonmarriage" manner.)

(Anointing and/or Laying on of hands)
Leader: Receive the blessing of Jesus and the power of the presence of God in your new life. Go from here renewed and strengthened for your journey.

Blessing for Remarriage

<u>Comments:</u> More and more people are marrying for the second or third time. Each wedding should be honored as a sincere commitment to a hopeful dream and affirmed as a covenant between the parties and with God. However, if issues from previous marriages have gone unresolved, there is danger ahead.

In cases where the marriage partners still carry unresolved issues from a previous marriage, the one who will convey a blessing on the next marriage may wish to utilize all or part of the divorce ritual on page 55 prior to offering a blessing for entering into another covenant relationship. This is a matter of pastoral care and provides an additional opportunity to deal with the participants and any "baggage" they may yet be carrying from their former unions. Each situation should be approached with special care, and every effort should be made to reach a sense of resolution for previous issues, which will allow for a more complete understanding of the dissolution of the previous covenant. Following the use of some aspect of the divorce ritual, a simple blessing or the appropriate parts of the premarital blessing on page 51 should be used.

If previous marriage issues have been resolved to the participants' satisfaction, the premarital blessing, with adjustments for the "second time around," could be used.

58

BLESSING FOR A FIRST JOB

<u>Comments:</u> Vocation is part of God's gift to us. We are all blessed with different and unique talents and skills, and it is pleasing to God when we are able to actually use these gifts in our chosen vocations. When employment is seen as a part of God's blessings, the workplace is better framed as one of the locations for ministry in daily life.

Items Needed: *The person brings a symbol of their new job. This could be a briefcase, a nurse's cap, a shovel, whatever they have chosen for the ritual. If anointing is planned, prepare the oil beforehand.*

Leader: Finding God's will for your life has been part of your task as you have grown up. Today we celebrate a new start, the beginning of your work/vocation of _____. In this work you will have opportunities to serve God through the use of your gifts and talents, and we commend this work to you and the Holy Spirit.

In addition, in this new place of work you will meet many people who are in need of Christ. It is part of your baptismal calling to be a priest to them, hearing their fears, sharing their pains, working with them for justice: being Christ to your coworkers. It is a privilege to work for God through our vocation, and we celebrate with you this opportunity.

You have chosen _____ to symbolize your new job. Please tell why you have chosen this as a symbol of the work that you will begin. *(The person shares the meaning of the symbol.)*

(With anointing/laying on of hands)
Leader: _____ , I bless you in the name of Jesus Christ to God's service. You have been called as a priest and as a _____ , and we ask God's blessing and the power of the Holy Spirit to empower you for your task.

BLESSING UPON RETIREMENT

Comments: Often spouses are heard to say that their retired partners are "driving them crazy!" By lifting up retirement as a time to do God's work in different ways and often at different speeds, we can affirm the gifts and talents that may have been underused or completely hidden until a person finds new time and new purpose for his or her vocation. We all love to be needed, and sometimes retirement is viewed as a burden due to the lack of job-related identity. The ritual preparation provides a great opportunity for pastoral care and conversation around plans for the retirement years. This ritual is also appropriate for persons who have been "downsized/laid off/let go" with minimal changes in the wording.

Items Needed: Often it is helpful to administer a "Spiritual Gifts inventory" (many are available) to assist the person in redirecting their energies and talents. There are those who honestly are not aware of their giftedness in those areas which are so apparent to others: exhortation, mercy, justice, helping, prayer, service, giving. These "soft gifts" are often overlooked in favor of the "hard gifts" of craftsmanship, administration, teaching, or building. In other words, it might just be the unique task of the church to lift up and affirm the gifts of the Spirit which are more ontological, that is, those gifts of "being," rather than concentrating solely on talents and skills, the gifts of "doing." As author John Bradshaw says, "we are 'human beings' not 'human doings'!" This exploration might be extremely effective in helping people redirect their focus for the future. The inventory results may be used as part of this ritual, along with the symbol chosen by the participant and oil for anointing, if desired.

Leader: We gather in the name of the Father, and of the Son, and of the Holy Spirit. Amen.

(A symbol of the life now past is chosen and brought forward by the participant/s.)

You have come here today to reaffirm your commitment to God's care of you as you undergo a life transition. Often our lives are rearranged by circumstances for which we see no good reason. Other times we choose a new path, a new direction for ourselves by our words, deeds, and accomplishments. Either way, your life is precious to God and has abundant meaning, especially within this community, which is one expression of the body of Christ on earth.

(The participant may share the meaning behind the symbol brought.)

Leader: You have shared with us the importance of the symbol of your former career/vocation/task. Today we celebrate the years given to you in the ministry of that portion of your life, and we turn our attention to the new life to come.

(Some "results/ideas" from the inventory may be shared.)

_____ , you have been called to the service of God through the waters of Baptism. In those waters God claimed you forever as a child of God and a minister of the gospel. As you approach this new adventure ahead, may God's Spirit empower you to see yourself as a treasured partner in the work in the vineyard of God's kingdom. May God strengthen you for service, always mindful of being a good steward of the gifts you have been given from the time you were knit together in your mother's womb. May you always find ways to share these gifts for the lifting up of the body of Christ.

(Use with the laying on of hands and/or anointing for special tasks or service)

Leader: _____ , I bless you in the name of Jesus Christ our Lord, and I ask you to remember that you have been called out to be a minister of the gospel in all that you say and do.

Let us rejoice together with _____ at the new adventure on which he/she is about to embark.

(To be included if the blessing is done in a public setting.)
Leader: People of God, I ask you, will you affirm _____'s continuing ministry by keeping him/her in your prayers, and strengthen him/her by your encouragement in this new endeavor? If so, answer, **"We will."**

Leader: The peace of the Lord be with you always.
All: And also with you.

CHAPTER THREE

Daily Living

Blessing Rituals for Everyday Life

In my ministry I have found that there are a variety of circumstances and occasions where blessing rituals can remind the community that we are connected to God in everyday living. These opportunities are abundant and reinforce the celebratory nature of life together in Christ. Some of the following rituals are for specific occasions, while others can be used daily or made available for members of the community with minimal explanation and direction. In this way they will have the framework for creating their own blessings within the context of their own unique life situations. I am convinced that continual blessing belongs within the context of praise and unceasing prayer.

Affirming/Recommitting to Faith

<u>Comments:</u> Often, especially with young adults, I have encountered the question of being "born again," in the sense of a deeper commitment to Christ. When young persons find their own personal experience of God they may wish to recommit themselves in a special way. The temptation (within my Lutheran context) is to commingle our doctrinal understanding of being "born again" through the waters of Baptism with believer's baptism or a conscious act of commitment (often beyond Confirmation). Although we confess in the Nicene Creed that "we believe in one baptism for the forgiveness of sins," it is the act of Baptism that is desired. The following ritual uses a familiar baptismal format and symbols, but does not rebaptize the person wishing to recommit his or her life. It differs from available "Affirmation of Baptism" liturgies in that it is less formal and more geared to the recommitment.

Items Needed: Review this ritual and gather those items which you choose to incorporate: hymnals or songbooks, oil (if anointing is part of your use of this ritual), baptismal information from the participant(s) such as place and date of their Baptism and names of sponsors. If desired, the sponsors may be invited.

(A hymn/song may be sung as the group gathers around the font. "Take My Life, That I May Be" is a good one.)
Leader: We remind ourselves of our Baptism each day as we make the sign of the cross. Therefore we begin this service in the name of the Father, and of the Son, and of the Holy Spirit. Amen.

_____ , you have expressed a desire to come closer to Jesus Christ, having made your own personal and unique decision to live as a child of God in this world. In our recent conversations you have shared with me your experience, and the Holy Spirit has stirred up in you a new yearning for the heart of God.

(At this point you may share some of the conversation, as appropriate, or the person may wish to share the story personally.)

We celebrate with you the dawning of this new day. For on this day you truly apprehend for yourself the relationship which God began in you at your Baptism which took place at *(place of Baptism)* on *(date of Baptism)*.

(If parents and sponsors are in attendance, they should be mentioned as well and thanked for their commitment to the raising of this person in the Body of Christ. The person may wish to bestow a small gift as a token at this time.)

On that day, you were baptized in water, which nourishes all living things. You may also have been anointed with oil, as a sign of the Holy Spirit.

(In churches that anoint during Baptism and commemorate Ash Wednesday with the imposition of ashes, the following section may be used.)

Today we remember and affirm those actions by tracing the sign of the cross in water upon your forehead, in the same spot that was anointed with oil so many years ago to remind you to whom you belong—and the same spot that each year receives the cross of ashes to remind you to whom you will return.

Today we anoint your hands and your lips with oil.

(As the lips are touched with oil)

May the words of your lips and the meditations of your heart be acceptable in God's sight, and may God's Word be like honey to you.

(As the palms of the hands are anointed with crosses of oil, some words about the person's vocation may be shared either by the pastor or by the parent or sponsors.)

(Portions of a commitment hymn may be sung or said, for example, "Take my hands and let them move, at the impulse of thy love" from "Take My Life That I May Be.")

Leader: Now let us all join together in blessing this newly committed Christian for renewed service within the Body of Christ:
(The Aaronic Benediction [Num. 6:24-26] or another may be used.)

> The LORD bless you and keep you;
> The LORD make his face to shine upon you
>   and be gracious to you;
> The LORD lift up his countenance upon you,
> And give you peace. Amen.

Leader: The peace of the Lord be with you always.
All: And also with you.

Blessing of the Backpacks/Lunchboxes

<u>Comments:</u> This service, developed for use at an annual "worship in the park," has been used by several colleagues for the past few years. It is celebrated a few weeks prior to the beginning of school, often on Rally Day. This blessing may be inserted during the Children's Time, or immediately following the Hymn of the Day. Include a blessing for a collection of school supplies for children in need.

Items Needed: *Plan on publicizing the service well so that the little ones have plenty of time to complete their school shopping and bring their lunchboxes, backpacks, gym bags, etc. to the worship service in the park.*

Leader: We have gathered these children and these items together today in thanksgiving for the gift of education.

Let us pray: In thanksgiving for students and teachers, helpers and school administrators, for coaches and staff we come before you, Almighty God, and seek your blessing.

Today our youngsters bring before God their lunchboxes, notebooks, and backpacks, that these may be blessed and dedicated to the glory of God. We also dedicate these school kits and supplies, assembled by the children of _____ church for the use of _____ *(service organization)* as they seek to do your work with school children in various parts of the state/country/world.

All of us, your servants, bless you, Lord, God of earth, for your love and your glory. Guide us in your ways, and give us the gifts of your Holy Spirit to do your work in our everyday lives. Amen.

BLESSING OF THE ANIMALS
ST. FRANCIS OF ASSISI FEAST DAY
(OCTOBER 4)

Comments: I had been aware of the existence of this practice in Roman Catholic and Episcopal circles for many years. Since our community is very young and has lots of children (and therefore lots of pets) I wanted to provide this opportunity within our context. I sought in vain for a ritual and, finding none that were satisfactory for our situation, wrote this one. Note: Since we also have a number of veterinarians in our congregation, we offer "wellness checks" at the same time; in this way we hope to emphasize a holistic approach to health in a different sort of venue. (And I have never had a dog or dog/cat disagreement during the ritual—I think they understand what's going on!)

―――∞∞∞――

Items Needed: If at all possible, weather permitting, hold this brief ritual outside. If you are in a location that is highly visible to the neighborhood, "dress" the space with banners, etc. In addition, local newspapers love the photo opportunities presented by a gathering of children, animals, and vested clergy!

Leader: We gather in the name of our Creator: Father, Son, and Holy Spirit. Amen.

(The opening verses of Genesis 1 are read—I sometimes encourage the children ahead of time to find and bring verses from scripture that mention animals.)

God has given us companions of many types to help us walk through this life. Many of you have brought these faithful companions to God to be blessed for the coming year. It is right to remember that God, who has created all living things, continues to bless life in all forms, and us with their very existence. As I move through the crowd and individually bless each animal, please introduce your pets to one another.

_____ , I bless you in the name of our Creator. May you be a faithful companion to your family, and lead a long and healthy life in their midst.

(You might wish to close with "Let All Things Now Living," "All Creatures of Our God and King," or other appropriate creation song.)

BLESSINGS "TO GO"
(MARISSA'S BLESSING)

<u>Comments:</u> In our community, everyone comes weekly to the altar rail to receive Holy Communion or a blessing. When one of our young ones was unable to attend for some period of time (the absence might be for many reasons: illness, injury, or shared custody), I perceived two things: both that I missed that young one, and that the family members were painfully aware of the separation at that particular moment in the service. As I approached one father, kneeling with hands resting open on the rail, I took one of his hands and made the sign of the cross in his palm. "Take this home to Marissa," I said. He did. I have often repeated this little ritual, especially with children, who are given the mission of "take this home to your mommie" (or Grandpa or other "missing person"). When someone is absent, they are reminded that they are missed.

Morning Good-Byeing
(At Home or Daycare)

<u>Comments:</u> Many working parents find themselves faced with the difficult daily task of saying good-bye to their children while they are cared for by someone other than a parent. While we all know avoiding good-byes is not healthy, often parents try to wait till the child is distracted, then slip away. Kathleen Szaj, in her book *I Hate Goodbyes!* advises that instead you should agree that this is a sad time and that you will miss each other during the day, but that you will be very happy to see each other again later.[1]

Szaj suggests that making up a silly ritual, like singing a little song together ("So long, farewell, auf wiedersehen, good-night" from *The Sound of Music* comes immediately to mind) or having a secret handshake and hug are ways to mark the good-bye privately just between you two. Agreeing to think about each other at a special time is another way of working through the parting. To say good-bye to young readers, pass them a brief letter to read whenever they wish during the day. Prereaders would be just as happy with a little drawing made just for them.

PET FUNERAL

<u>Comments:</u> In a congregation which is mostly families with small children, there are many pets (see also Blessing of the Animals). Most families deal with the death of a family pet by burying the animal in an appropriate space with appropriate sentiments spoken, or perhaps even a prayer of committal. I wanted to provide a ritual that would express not only the concern of the pastor (and, by extension, of the church) at the loss of a special friend but in some cases a new way to connect the pastor or church leader, parishioners, and pet to the theological "whole" of Christian life together. The preparations for this service are best done with the children. Make it a point to discuss with them your own beliefs or the beliefs of your church about heaven and the afterlife. Even if you do not believe that little Fido will be yapping at the Pearly Gates, this is a great opportunity to explore God's love for all of the creation, and God's desire for care and stewardship of all the blessings we have been given.

Items Needed: *This ritual can be done at the actual burial, or later as a memorial. It is helpful, for the children especially, to gather the pet's accessories that will no longer be used. One way to open the ritual is to think together about what should be done with these symbols of the companion now gone.*

Leader: We are gathered today in the presence of our Creator to remember our friend, _____.

(Anyone who wishes may share a story, a memory or their thoughts about the pet. If the body of the pet is present, it may be placed in the ground and covered with flower petals, leaves, evergreen boughs, or other natural materials before being covered with dirt. It is important that the children see the burial. The

grave may be marked with a stone decorated by the children, a small cross, or flowers.)
(Include a reading from Scripture here. The Creation story, Noah filling the Ark, the 23rd Psalm, or other scripture which high-lights animals would be appropriate.)

Let's pray together. Heavenly God and Gracious Creator, we are here today to bless each other and the memory of our companion _____. We thank you for creating him/her and for blessing this home with his/her companionship and love. We know that your care for every living thing extends beyond this earth, and we ask that you would comfort this family at this time of parting. Let our grief come naturally and depart quickly, but allow us the warm memories of our time together and the special love we shared. Strengthen us to give that same love again to our other pets, those we currently care for, and those that are to come. Thank you for the time we shared together, and bless _____ with your eternal love. Amen.

VOCATIONAL BLESSINGS

<u>Comments:</u> A parishioner came to me after completing her nursing degree. She had waited until her kids were grown and then returned to school in nursing as a second career. Because she had so intentionally chosen nursing as a profession, she wanted to ritualize her new career within the church. One Sunday following a regular worship service we gathered in the sanctuary for the blessing ceremony.

Items Needed: Any vocation can be lifted up in this way using a few Bible verses, a prayer specific to the work of the vocation, a symbol chosen by the participant, and an anointing which is connected to the service to be performed. See "Blessing for Youth on Retreat" on page 78 to get ideas for other vocational anointings.

Leader: We begin in the name of the Father, and of the Son, and of the Holy Spirit. Amen.

Creator God, we ask for your blessing on _____ as she begins a new phase of her service to you. You who are the Great Physician, we ask that you be present with her as she goes about the work of healing and caring for those in pain and distress.

Give her patience and energy to perform her ministry among your people. Keep her always mindful of the privilege she has been given to do the same kind of ministry that you yourself performed when you walked among us on earth.

Bless this cap and pin, symbols of her position as a nurse. Bless her as she wears these symbols and performs her ministry, the work of healing.

We anoint her hands as gifts from you, and ask that you receive her service as she gives it, with joy and thanksgiving for a vocation full of meaning. May the tasks never become a burden, but always remind her that each small task done *"to one of the least of these . . ."* has been done for you (Matt. 25:40).

Go and heal in the peace given to you by our risen Lord and Savior, Jesus Christ.

BLESSING FOR CHURCH MUSICIANS

(In liturgical worship settings, use immediately following the Hymn of the Day.)

Leader: At this time we would like to recognize and affirm the music ministry at this church. Would all those who are involved in the music ministry of this congregation please stand where you are.

Leader: A reading from Paul's First Letter to the Corinthians, chapter 12, verses 4-7: "Now there are varieties of gifts, but the same Spirit; and there are varieties of services, but the same Lord; and there are varieties of activities, but it is the same God who activates all of them in everyone. To each is given the manifestation of the Spirit for the common good."

Leader: I ask you now to confirm that you will be faithful in the service of the Lord within this congregation by sharing your gifts of music. Will you promise to lead this community in our praise of God, to lift up the gospel in its purity through music, and to continually strive to enhance our worship by sharing your gifts of music? If so, answer, **"We will."**

Leader: Congregation, I ask you: Will you support these musicians and their creative ministry through prayer and thanksgiving? If so, answer, **"We will."**

Leader: Readings from Psalms 146-50:

Praise the LORD!
I will praise the LORD as long as I live;
   I will sing praises to my God all my life long. (146:1*a*, 2)

How good it is to sing praises to our God;
    for he is gracious, and a song of praise is fitting. (147:1*b*)

Sing to the LORD a new song,
    his praise in the assembly of the faithful. (149:1*b*)

Let everything that breathes praise the LORD! (150:6)

(Other prayers of the church may be inserted here.)

Leader: At this time I invite _____ , our Director of Music, and _____ , our organist, to come forward for the laying on of hands. *(Invite them to kneel for the laying on of hands. You might also wish to anoint the palms and/or hands.)*
    _____ , I bless you in the name of Jesus Christ our Lord, to serve God faithfully with your leadership, your guidance, and your creative gifts. Amen.
    _____ , I bless you in the name of Jesus Christ our Lord, to serve God faithfully with your leadership, your guidance, and your creative gifts. Amen.

On behalf of this assembly, carry this blessing *(and anointing)* to all who work with you to bring glory to God through your created gifts and faithful service.

(You may conclude with the sharing of the peace.)

BLESSING FOR YOUTH ON RETREAT

Comments: At the conclusion of a vocation-themed youth retreat, we did a final blessing for each young person's self-identified spiritual gift. For some, the question of identifying their gift/talent was limited by a secular understanding. The goal was to highlight their "earthly" talents as gifts from God, which can be used within the context of their daily ministry. After the greeting at our closing Eucharist service, I called every young person forward to be anointed for service in accordance with the gift or talent that each had identified for himself or herself. Be prepared with a variety of applicable scriptures, and the Spirit will help you apply them to any talent named. Here are a few to get you started:

For the soccer player (anointing the tops of the feet): *"Blessed are the feet of those who bring the gospel of peace"* (Rom. 10:15). May your whole body celebrate the gift of life and strength that has been given to you by our Creator. May you use your gifts to the glory of the one who "first knew you, knitting you together in your mother's womb," and may you always seek ways to bring the good news of God's love through Jesus into the lives of those with whom you work and play and live.

For the scholar (anointing the forehead): *"Love the Lord your God with all your heart, with all your soul, with all your mind, with all your strength"* (Mark 12:30). Blessings on the gift of your intellect. Never allow those who are jealous of this gift make you regret your brainpower, but use it for study and to teach others of the wonders of God's universe and the love of its Creator for the creation.

For the debater (anointing the lips): *"May the words of my mouth and the meditations of my heart be acceptable in your sight, O Lord"* (Ps. 19:14). Blessings on your ability to persuade and to speak to others in the language of God's love. May you always be challenged to find ways to convey the gospel to those who have not yet heard of the saving acts of Jesus.

BLESSING RITUALS FOR BEGINNING AND END OF RETREAT

Comments: For our annual women's retreat, I like to include a number of symbols and rituals that are created as we go along. This particular retreat was organized around the theme of "Spiritual Gifts from the Church and to the Church." We began by identifying the gifts God has given our own faith journeys and ended by anointing each retreatant, lifting up and affirming the gifts that we perceived in each other. The retreat was attended by people who already knew one another, so the gathering ritual took on a deeper dimension than just a "get to know you" exercise.

Items Needed: To begin, place a number of readily available religious symbols in a central location that everyone can see. We used a shell, a small wooden cross, and a lighted candle. It is wise to have tissues available, as often this kind of sharing leads to deep emotions.

Leader: Tonight we begin to get to know one another better by sharing some thoughts about what gifts God has given to us through the church. I would like each one of us to choose one of the items in the center of our circle and share why we are especially drawn to that symbol. This can be a story, a memory, or what the symbol means for your life.

(After all the stories, memories, etc. are shared, take a moment of quiet contemplation. Chances are there have been some emotions shared with the stories; let their power carry you into and through the silence.)

Let's pray together. Creator God, you who have knit us together in our mother's wombs and have known us as your precious children, keep us safe through this night.

Prepare our hearts to receive you anew in the morning light and always see all that we are as your gift to us. It is our delight and our intent to return these gifts to you. We pray these things in Jesus' name. Amen.

(For the closing ritual, have oil available in a baptismal shell, pyx, or other appropriate container. By anointing each other, the participants feel more closely linked to one another and to our doctrinal understanding of the "priesthood of all believers.")

Leader: This brings us to the end of our retreat time together. Before we go to our individual homes and our separate lives, let's take time to lift up for each other the gifts that we have seen and experienced in the stories and the activities during this time apart from our everyday lives. I have prepared oil for anointing and would invite you to think for a moment about the person to your right. What have you learned about her gifts this weekend? What have you experienced in her ministry at church? How might you best affirm her special talents and where would that talent symbolically reside in her body, for the purposes of anointing? Let's take a few moments in silent reflection, and then I will begin.
(The anointing should be done thoughtfully and without rushing.)

Leader: Our time together in this place has come to a close. May God bless your departure and your travel home. May you carry in your heart the love of Christ that has been shared here today. And may the Holy Spirit empower your service as you seek always to share the gifts that God has multiplied in the unique and precious person that God has created as you.

Leader: Go in peace! Serve the Lord!
All: Thanks be to God!

VIGIL OF PENTECOST

<u>Comments:</u> My church celebrates the Triduum (The Three Days of Maundy Thursday, Good Friday, and the Great Vigil of Easter), and it seems only fitting that we should find some intentional ways to celebrate Pentecost, the birthday of the church, in a more liturgical fashion. Just as we gathered to await the resurrection, we gather again with the disciples in the city to wait for the "clothing of power from on high." Ritual symbols to be used are wind and fire and anything that will work for the cacophony of languages. The following is patterned on the Easter Vigil.

Items Needed: *The sanctuary is still vested in the white/gold of the Easter season. One suggestion for heightening the anticipation and maintaining visual interest throughout the Easter season is to add new flowers as the lilies fade. Our church typically moves from the white of the lilies to yellows, then to peaches and oranges, and finally, on Pentecost Sunday, to flaming reds. Usually, the nurseries and greenhouses offer an abundance of mums, daisies, salvia, and other appropriately colored spring annuals. Invite different families to add plants to the flower arrangement each week and then, following their use in worship, plant them at the church or in their own gardens. Have the following items preset in the rear of the church or in the sacristy: red vestments and paraments; preparation for Holy Communion; other decorative items for use in the morning Festival of Pentecost services (i.e., red balloons, banners, streamers, etc.). Our sanctuary artisans regularly devise new ways to "surprise" the vigil-ers with their handiwork. Banners sometimes "appear" from the ceiling, from beneath the altar, or from behind curtains. It is quite dramatic, and great fun. Review this ritual for other items you choose to include.*

The congregation gathers in the narthex, and the Christ candle, lighted before anyone enters, is brought from the sanctuary to the narthex. This candle, lighted from the "new fire" struck at the Easter Vigil, leads the worshipers to the font for the affirmation of Baptism.

(The following is intoned on one pitch, three separate times; each set is intoned one step higher.)

Leader: The light of Christ.

All: Thanks be to God! *(repeat twice more)*

(At the font, a service of affirmation of Baptism is performed. You may use one from your denominational service book or something similar. An example follows.)

Leader: When you came to the waters of Baptism, whether as an infant or more fully grown, you were joined to the death and resurrection of our Lord and Savior Jesus Christ. Water has always been a sign of freedom, of cleansing and of rebirth. In this water, you were freed from the bondage of death, cleansed from your sins and reborn as precious children of God. Tonight we affirm our status of being claimed by Christ, as we join together in the ancient words of the Nicene Creed:

(The Nicene Creed is recited by all. In noncreedal churches, substitute an appropriate prayer.)

Leader: Rejoicing in the new life given to us in these waters, and remembering each day that we have been born again, we gather tonight to recall not only the gift of the Holy Spirit which was given to us in our Baptism but also that special day so long ago when the disciples were "clothed with power from on high," and displayed the Holy Spirit's greatness on the Day of Pentecost, the birthday of the church.

All: Amen. Come Holy Spirit, come to us.

Stories from Scripture are read. You may select from the readings appointed for the Easter Vigil or for the Vigil of Pentecost or from others with baptismal and/or Holy Spirit themes. The final reading before midnight should be from Acts 2, and is especially effective if individual candles are lighted to be held by each worshiper. During the reading, appropriate sounds may be made, using pebbles in a pie plate, rainsticks, or other "rattling" types of noisemakers. If wind sounds can be played, all the better; if not, invite the worshipers to assist. (Children really like this part!)

Leader: The Spirit of God is upon us! The church is born. Come, Lord Jesus, come!
All: Come and dwell with us, Holy Spirit!
Leader: Come, Lord Jesus, come!
All: Empower our lives this night!

As midnight strikes, invite the worshipers to bring forward the red paraments, flowers and other decorations for the celebration of Pentecost. Set the altar for Holy Communion and celebrate. Following communion offer this prayer:
Leader: The Lord be with you.
All: And also with you.
Leader: Let us pray. Almighty and ever living God, we give you thanks that you sent your Son to live among us and to show us the way. Through the power of his Spirit, give us the strength and the courage to carry the good news of your love to all who have not heard. Teach us to be always ready to witness to what you have done for us, through the grace of your goodness. We pray these things in the name of Jesus Christ, our Lord and our Savior.
All: Amen.

A closing hymn may be sung.

Leader: Let us go forth in the power of the Spirit.
All: Thanks be to God!

ALL SEASONS LITURGY

(For use late in the season of Pentecost or on Christ the King Sunday)

Comments: Having always been personally nourished by the cycles of the church seasons, I wanted to develop a narrated liturgy as a teaching tool for the congregation. Imagine my delight when I discovered that the order of the church seasons are roughly equivalent to the order of the mass! The following is my version.

Items Needed: *The sanctuary is vested either with no paraments or paraments are present for each color/season of the church year. If paraments are changed, an asterisk [*] marks the point in the service at which it is time to do so.*

Announcements

Leader: Welcome to worship this morning! Today we are doing things a little differently. As you look at the bulletin you will see that our "normal" Sunday liturgy has been divided into sections, each designated as a "season" or a "festival day." As we go through the service, you will see the similarities between the flow of our worship, which is based on the Latin mass, and the liturgical calendar. In other words, as the worship service goes, so goes the "Church Year."

Today is designated as Christ the King Sunday, the final Sunday of the season of Pentecost and the last Sunday of the church year. Next week we begin the annual cycle again, as we move into a new church year, which begins with the season of Advent. We thought it would be interesting to "review" the past year (liturgically speaking), so that you can see how our Sunday worship reflects the whole cycle and so that you can get a sense of the "flow" of the seasons of the church.

The first half of our church year focuses on the life, death, and resurrection of Jesus of Nazareth, our Savior and our Lord. In the second half of the year the focus shifts to the church and the members of the Body of Christ as we seek to live out lives of service to the one who comes into history and into each of our lives. And so the new year and our worship begin, as we remember that **blue** signifies preparation and waiting: the color of Advent. *(The altar candles are lighted; then the 4 Advent candles on the wreath.* Amend the color in the narration if purple/pink candles are used for Advent.)*

Entrance Hymn—*"O Come, O Come, Emmanuel" (verses 1, 3, and 5)*

Apostolic Greeting

Leader: The community has gathered to await the coming Messiah. We stand in the fields with the shepherds and search the night sky for the promised sign, the symbol that announces his birth. In the darkest hour, a brilliant star appears. The precious child who has come into our lives to save us from our sinful natures has been born in a small rural community on the outskirts of the holy city of Jerusalem. A baby cries in Bethlehem, and the heavens rejoice at his coming. It is *Christmas, the Nativity of our Lord, Jesus,* and the colors are **white and gold.** *(The Paschal candle is lighted.*)*

Hymn of Praise—*"Hark! the Herald Angels Sing"*

The Prayer of the Day *(as appointed for the Sunday you are celebrating)*

Leader: As a community of faith we celebrate the coming of Christ by looking to the star that symbolizes his birth on *the Day of the Epiphany.* Epiphany means "revealing," for it was the star, the heavenly messenger that led the wise men, the kings, from their homes in the east to the place where Jesus was born. Here their journey ended, and their dreams were fulfilled. As they knelt before the Christ Child, they presented precious gifts of gold, frankincense, and myrrh.

Selected verses from *"We Three Kings"*

Leader: Even the Son of God met the expectation of cultural traditions and fulfilled all that was required of good Jews: his family adhered to the custom of presenting their boy in the Temple and circumcision on the eighth day; Jesus presented himself for baptism in the river Jordan. We observe similar rituals to mark the passages in our lives and the lives of our children. We remind ourselves in our scripture readings that God is the author of all our days and that we are to continue to seek ways for every gift to be put to use in the building up of the Body of Christ, and to further the coming of God's kingdom on earth.

First Lesson—Ecclesiastes 3:1-8

Psalm 63:1-8

(The Paschal candle is extinguished.*)

Leader: Nurtured by the Holy Scriptures, we take some time to grow. **Green** marks *the season of Epiphany,* and just as Jesus matured from infancy into childhood into manhood, we pause amid the cold of winter to ponder our own spiritual growth and how God is working through us. We ask the same questions Jesus must have asked about life: "Why am I here?" "What would God have me do with all the gifts I have been given?" "What is God's plan for my life?"

Leader: We feel an urgency as we try to perceive what God has called us to do. Just as Jesus sought to understand what God wanted from his life and work, we are constantly searching after God and God's plan for us. We know that Jesus will return to take us to himself, and we try to use our gifts to fulfill God's desire for us as we grow toward heaven.

The Gospel (or Second) Lesson—Matthew 25:1-13; Luke 19:1-10; 1 Peter 2:2-5

Temple Talk or Homily

Hymn of the Day—*"Oh, That the Lord Would Guide My Ways"*

Leader: *The Epiphany season is a time for seeking, for growing, for connecting with God to strengthen our journey of faith for the hard times that come to any human life. For each of us, as for all of God's children, there comes a time in life when we accept for ourselves the message of salvation promised in Baptism, and we take our place in the community of the faithful. Just as Christ was confirmed as the Messiah in the **white**ness of God's glory on *the Day of Transfiguration,* we confirm our faith each time we state the ancient words about who we are and what we believe. This creed reminds us that we are family, the Body of Christ in this world.

The Apostles' Creed
The Prayer of the Church
The Sharing of the Peace (*)

Leader: The season changes, and in Jesus' life and ministry, "he set his face toward Jerusalem." The forty days of repentance, reflection, and renewal we experience during Lent mirror other Bible accounts of forty: the forty years the Israelites spent wandering in the wilderness and the forty days of temptation Jesus endured after his baptism.

We begin the Lenten journey with the **black** of *Ash Wednesday,* when we are reminded once again of our own mortality with the imposition of ashes and the words "Remember that you are dust, and into dust you shall return." Ash Wednesday focuses our attention on the fact of our own death, and points us to the reality that all that we are, all we have, all we achieve will one day be dust. Ash Wednesday moves us beyond the futility of a life spent for "nothing" toward the freedom of a life poured out in service to others for God's sake.

A Brief Order for Confession and Forgiveness

Leader: For the gifts that God has given us and the gratitude we feel because God gives our very lives their meaning and purpose, we return a portion of ourselves, our time and our possessions to God through our tithes and our offerings.

The Offering
Offering Hymn—*"Take My Life, That I May Be"*
Offertory Prayer

Leader: *Now fully into *the Season of Lent*, we focus on the royal color of penitence, which is **purple,** and we ponder who we are as God's people. We take time to renew our spiritual relationship with God and we begin preparations for remembering his Passion, his suffering and death; always mindful of how grateful we are that death now claims no victory over us because of Jesus Christ, God's loving sacrifice.

The Great Thanksgiving
   (option) *The Proper Preface for Lent
   (option) *"Holy, Holy, Holy"*
The Eucharistic Prayer
The Lord's Prayer
The Agnus Dei—*"Lamb of God"*
The Distribution of Holy Communion
The Post-Communion Blessing

Leader: Now we have shared with Christ his body and blood. We have watched his death by Crucifixion and waited through the nights that he lay dead in a stone-cold tomb. We breathe in the pain that our sinfulness has caused God, and we look to the heavens for an answer to our despair.

Leader: We walk to the tomb with the women, our hearts full of sorrow—but wait! The tomb is empty and an angel proclaims that even the powers of evil and death cannot hold our Lord. "He is not here. He is risen!" God has won the victory! It is Easter, *the Resurrection of our Lord,* and even the **white, gold,** and lilies of creation cannot express the joy we feel as the dawn of Christ breaks into our weary hearts.

(The Paschal candle is lighted.*)
   Post-Communion Canticle—*"Jesus Christ Is Risen Today! Alleluia!"*
   Post-Communion Prayer

(The Paschal candle light is taken by a baptismal candle to the font. The Paschal candle is extinguished.*)

Leader: The light and the power of Christ are shared with each of us in the waters of our Baptism, and we are reminded that we, the followers of Jesus the Christ, have work to do. Our Lord has returned to his heavenly Father and left us with the assignment to "Go and tell everyone the good news about what God has done for you."

On the *Day of Pentecost,* as the disciples gathered in the city of Jerusalem to preach the gospel of forgiveness and teach the people about Jesus, there was a sound like the rush of a mighty wind, and tongues like fire descended upon them from heaven. And they were "clothed with power from on high." The color is **red,** the intensity of fire.

In our baptism, we received the heavenly strength to do the right thing, to speak the forgiving word, to bring comfort to the sick and grieving, and to proclaim justice to the lands.

   Hymn—*"Spirit of God, Descend Upon My Heart"* *(verses 1 and 4)*

Leader: *Renewed by God's Holy Word and by the nourishment of Christ's presence in the bread and wine, and reminded that we have been born again in the waters of Baptism and filled with the Holy Spirit, we, like the first disciples, are strengthened once again to go forth and live abundantly. Throughout the long **green** *Season of Pentecost,* we learn how to live out our unique ministries. We rejoice that God has so richly blessed us with the salvation that frees us to *be* hope and compassion in the midst of a despairing world. Through the ministry of our daily lives, we give thanks to God for all that we are, all that we have, and all that we are able to do for others, knowing that we are empowered by the Holy Spirit to do so, because God's promise of forgiveness and love will never fail.

The Benediction

Leader: You have been blessed to be a blessing! Now go into your daily world and share the peace of God's kingdom, the goodness of God's love, and the power of God's forgiveness with all who have not heard!

Recessional Hymn—"*On Our Way Rejoicing*"

Dismissal

CHAPTER FOUR

Letting Go

Blessing Rituals for Pastoral Care

Most of my counseling sessions have as their motivation a desire to heal, to return to some state of balance or normalcy, or to order chaos. When creating rituals for use in pastoral care, it has been helpful to focus on two separate aspects of a ritual process, namely the *symbolic action* which has the power to transform, as well as the *blessing action* that should follow it. The focus on healing by use of symbolic action is reinforced by the "new life" symbolized in the blessing, often using the laying on of hands. In this way, the ritual symbolic action will be sustained beyond the immediacy of its performance.

Because of these two dimensions of the ritual process, it is important to pay attention to incorporating *both* aspects into each ritual action that is created. This roots the entire ritual process in that recurring scriptural theme, *death and resurrection,* and ensures that the participants will not be left in their Good Friday but will be pointed intentionally to the new life promised in Easter.

In the following rituals it is assumed that the counselor is an ordained person. If that is not the case, these rituals should be done with both the professional staff counselor and the pastor present if possible. If a sacrament is included, then the presence of a pastor is required.

Blessing Ritual for a Broken Trust

"Building a Stronger House"

Comments: A parishioner confessed that he had had an extramarital affair. His marriage subsequently was in serious jeopardy, and he struggled with why his affair must end when it seemed so much more fulfilling than his marriage. As he began to recognize the symptoms which brought him to the place where an affair could happen, he chose to relinquish the affair and recommit himself to his spouse. In joint counseling, the couple decided to do whatever was necessary to work through the pain of healing their broken trust. Their anger, pain, and fear are indicators that the foundation underlying the marriage itself is now cracked and may never be solid again.

For those who desire to rebuild after an extramarital affair, the road is long and filled with potholes and deep trenches. This ritual is a helpful beginning for couples who have made a commitment to stay together and try again. Often these are folks for whom the covenant with God is very real, and they realize that it is only with God's assistance and the strength of the Holy Spirit that their marriage has a chance to be rebuilt. After counseling, then, when the themes of the destruction of trust have been explored and brought to the surface and the work to be done has been laid out, this ritual can serve as a point between the beginning of the healing and the ongoing work which will result in a stronger marriage.

—◦◦◦—

Items Needed: *Prior to this ritual, set the altar for a simple service of Holy Communion. Ensure that there is water in the baptismal font. The couple is brought into the sanctuary by the* *pastor and led to the font. Others who may have been invited by the couple should already be in their places.*

Leader: We begin the renewal of this relationship at the place of beginnings, the font which holds the water of Baptism. In your Baptisms, you were claimed by God as his precious children, and you have believed that God had a plan which included your relationship with one another.

Do you believe that God has called you together, to share your lives and your love with each other (and your family)? If so, answer, **"I do."**

Will you continue to seek God's strength and guidance as you rebuild your relationship in the coming years? If so, answer, **"I will."**

Leader: God has claimed you in this water, and loves you with a love that has no end. Receive the sign of the cross *(using water from the font)* upon your forehead as a reminder of that promise of love and of the presence of God's Holy Spirit in your lives.

Leader: *(at the altar)* At this table our Lord Jesus invites all who are burdened to come and be forgiven and nourished by his presence in the bread and the wine. At this time I ask you to confess to God and to one another (in the presence of this company) and to ask for God's forgiveness:

Spouse A: I, _____ , confess my sins and ask God to forgive me. And I ask you, _____ , to work with me to build a renewed relationship, grounded in trust and rooted in my love for you.

Spouse B: I, _____ , confess my sins and ask God to forgive me. And I promise you, _____ , to work with you on a renewed relationship, patiently learning to step out in trust and my love for you.

Leader: You have confessed your sins and promised your intentions. As a called and ordained minister, and by God's authority, I therefore declare to you the entire forgiveness of all your sins, in the name of the Father, and of the Son, and of the Holy Spirit. Amen.

As a sign of God's forgiveness and in celebration of the new creation in your love, we celebrate together this feast. As Jesus participated in the wedding feast at Cana, we now join together to receive his presence among us through this small taste of what is to come.

"On the night in which he was betrayed, our Lord Jesus took some bread in his hands, and blessed it and broke it and gave it to his friends saying, 'Take and eat, this is my body, given for you. Do this for the remembrance of me.'

"Again, after supper, he took the cup, and after giving thanks he gave it to them saying, 'Take this and drink. This cup is the new covenant in my blood, shed for you and for all people for the forgiveness of sins. Do this for the remembrance of me.' "[1]

The Lord's Prayer is said by all. The Pastor may commune the couple, who may then serve any gathered together.

Leader: And now may the body and blood of our Lord and Savior Jesus Christ strengthen you and keep you in his grace. Amen.

(The couple moves to the rail and kneels.)

You have come here today and been reminded of whose you are. You have been blessed by the water of Baptism and the bread and wine of Holy Communion. *(Lay on hands.)* Receive now the blessing of this community, as you move into a renewed relationship, a strengthened marriage, and a new life together. May God continue to bless you on your journey, with the knowledge that our Lord Jesus shared with all his disciples, "I am with you always, to the end of the age" (Matt. 28:20). Amen.

BLESSING RITUAL TO LET GO OF OLD GRIEF

"COMFORT ME, O GOD"

Comments: A member was concerned about a drinking problem but revealed that the underlying cause was a deep-seated grief that had never been resolved. This grief centered on the loss many years before of a loved one who had died, and the subsequent pain of attempting to live without the joy and comfort of his ongoing presence in her life. Others have sometimes grieved deeply over the loss of a place, even if the move was a decision that was made willingly and with great enthusiasm and excitement. However, the loss of community and surroundings that are deeply loved can initiate the same grieving process as the loss of a loved one.

Grief seems to be one of the most misunderstood processes of human existence. Unfortunately, many people believe that grieving is something to be avoided, as if ignoring it will simply make it go away. Tears are seldom shed in my presence without an accompanying apology. My response to these apologies is a quote I read many years ago which says, *"Don't chase your heart away."* By allowing someone to openly grieve, we allow them to feel the deep-seated emotion that has been kept inside, often for many years. It is a privilege to be "let in" by someone in counseling, and when the sessions look like they need to go beyond my standard "three visits, then refer" rule, I often recommend a ritual to soothe that passage from pastor to professional counselor. The following was written with the idea in mind that grief is simply the heart calling out to something wonderful that has passed and is deeply missed. This is not to be used when grieving is in response to tragic or harmful circumstance; for those situations, see the rituals for anger and resentment.

Gather in the sanctuary or other agreed-upon location with those involved (only at the invitation of the person for whom the ritual is being performed). The person should bring to the gathering a symbol of their choosing, representing the loss.

Pastor: We begin in the name of the Father, and of the Son, and of the Holy Spirit. Amen.

Let us pray. Creator God, source of life and health, we gather today in your presence with _____ , confident in your promise that "wherever two or more or gathered in your name, there you are in the midst of them." We ask that you might touch _____ with your healing and your peace, in the name of your gracious Son, Jesus Christ, our Lord. Amen.

(At this time, the person should review the source of the grief.)

_____ and I have come (to your altar) bearing a visible sign of the life/event which has long been the source of her/his grief. We offer it up to you (by placing it on your altar), and we ask that you would receive this symbol and replace its absence in her/his life with your special peace, "the peace that passes all understanding." *(The symbol is placed.)*

Pastor: Having relinquished the memory of this source of sorrow, let us celebrate together the life/event which is so greatly absent in the life of this child of God. Allow us to find together a new way to live in union with this memory, a way that provides comfort and healing whenever _____ recalls the joy which now seems lost forever.

Heal all of our past wounds, and bring us together again with those we love and those things we have lost in the glory of your eternal kingdom. We pray these things in Jesus' name, your Son, our Lord, who lives and reigns with you and the Holy Spirit. Amen.

(Discussion may follow as to the disposition of the symbol. It may be burned or buried or soaked in the soothing waters of the baptismal font—whatever seems appropriate to each individual's need.)

Pastor: Let us go forth in joy into the new creation that is this day. Blessings on your journey and on your capacity for love. May it bring you peace and comfort in the coming days. Amen.

BLESSING RITUAL TO RELEASE LONG-HELD ANGER

"UNBIND HIM, AND LET HIM GO"

Comments: A woman who had been the victim of incest many years ago had begun counseling for a completely different matter. When the abuse was identified, she was immediately referred to a professional abuse counselor. However, she was deeply concerned about the faith issues that were entangled in the years of anger held within. Letting go of anger is most effective when a person recognizes that anger usually masks a more powerful emotion like grief, hurt, or fear. The themes of cross and resurrection are most appropriate in helping people relinquish old pain. In addition, images of planting and pruning or of winter and spring would also be useful.

In contrast to the grief ritual, which is rooted in replacing feelings of sadness with loving memories of a person, place, or situation, the replacement of anger is often more difficult to achieve. Anger feeds upon itself and when retained will ravage the person in whom it resides. This ritual is intended for those whose anger is rooted in their own victimization (whether real or perceived).

Items Needed: Prior to the ritual, the person should choose a symbol to represent the event/person/place which is connected to the anger. Consider performing the ritual in a specific location. If appropriate, gather in the sanctuary or in a nearby cemetery. Unless other persons are intimately involved in this situation, limit this ritual to the person and the pastor. A Bible and anointing oil, if desired, should be available.

Pastor: We come together in the strong name of our Lord and Savior, Jesus Christ, who himself was nailed upon a cross for our sakes and suffered humiliation and pain on our behalf. *"Unless the seed fall into the ground and die, it will never bear fruit . . ."* (John 12:24, paraphrased).

(The person should briefly describe the anger and the source from which it stems.)

Pastor: _____ , do you fully intend to relinquish this anger, thereby giving God permission to heal your hurt and take away your pain? If so, answer, **"I do."**

As a called and ordained minister of the church, and by God's authority, and having heard your intention to let go of what has bound you, I declare you released from the bondage of this anger into the freedom of new life in Jesus Christ. Will you commit to the work that needs be done to continue your life free from this bondage? If so, answer, **"I will."**

Scripture Reading—*Choose any Gospel account of Jesus exorcising demons.*

(Briefly review some of the work to be done that has been discussed in counseling sessions. If others are present, do this at another time.)

Pastor: You have brought a symbol of your anger today. By disposing of this symbol, we imagine together an image of your anger being rid from your body as Jesus exorcised demons from so many of his faithful followers. *(Anointing an appropriate place on their person)* May this oil act as a healing balm to remind you that God wishes only good for his children, and that healing begins *today.* May it bless you and allow you to replace your anger with calm, your struggle with peace, and your pain with patience, in the name of Jesus Christ, our Lord. Amen.

BLESSING RITUAL FOR RELEASING RESENTMENT

"FREE AT LAST, FREE AT LAST . . ."

Comments: A disagreement had arisen between two parishioners. As the "objective observer" I felt the pain of the strained relationship and the underlying desire to make it better, although neither seemed to know how to take the first step. Issues of pride and territory were very much involved, and the decision to intervene seemed the only course for me to take.

Situations involving resentment are similar to those of anger, and often the two come together as a pair. The reading in the following ritual may include any Gospel account of an exorcism, the escape from slavery in Egypt, or John 8:31-36 *("The truth will make you free . . .")*. Emphasis should be placed on the promise of Jesus' power over evil in any form, as well as on resurrection themes.

Items Needed: Prior to the ritual, the participants should each choose a symbol to represent their resentment. The activity of choosing this symbol often takes care of the necessity for the ritual. As the participants seek to "embody" resentment, the physical symbol draws out the story, which is often all that the participants need: to tell their stories and have them heard. A Bible is needed.

Pastor: We gather together in the strong name of our Lord and Savior, Jesus Christ, who himself was nailed upon a cross and suffered to reconcile each of us to himself and to God.

(The participants should briefly describe their resentment and the source from which it stems.)

Pastor: _____ , do you fully intend to relinquish this resentment, thereby giving God permission to reconcile you with your brother/sister and begin to heal your hurt? If so, answer, **"I do."**

As a called and ordained minister of the church, by God's authority, and having heard your intention to let go of what has bound you, I declare you released from the restrictions of your resentment into the freedom of new life in Jesus Christ. Will you commit to the work that needs to be done to continue your life free from this bondage? If so, answer, **"I will."**

Scripture Reading—*Choose any Gospel account of Jesus reconciling two parties. Special attention might be given to the "continuing saga" of the prodigal son in Luke.*

Pastor: You have brought a symbol of your resentment. By disposing of this symbol, we ask God's blessing on your freedom to love your brother/sister again, and we celebrate together the reunion of members of the Body of Christ. Reconciled once again, we share the peace of the Lord with one another. *(A sign of peace is shared.)*

BLESSING RITUAL TO RELINQUISH INAPPROPRIATE LOVE
"COMMITTING TO WHAT IS REAL AND HEALTHY"

Comments: Often members come to me as they consider entering into an extramarital affair. Sometimes we begin with a "chat" on a different subject, and yet because God's time is always the right moment, their struggle will come into our discussion. Usually aware that what is being contemplated is not "the right thing to do," the temptation of feeling romance and love after many years of languishing in loveless marriages is extremely difficult to resist. In the best of all possible worlds, these people would find creative ways to recommit to their marriages, and the need for outside relationships would not seem so acute. Sadly, often that is not possible, and the cultural ritual of divorce is the outcome. But sometimes, a member decides to follow his or her conscience, to resist the temptation to stray, and to take intentional steps to avoid an affair. A ritual can be effective to assist in these first steps.

Letting go, as we have seen in most of these pastoral care rituals, is most easily accomplished when what we are relinquishing is replaced with something healthy. In the case of inappropriate love, the prayers should focus on strength to resist temptation. Because some marriages hold little hope of working out, the ritual task at hand becomes simply allowing the person to draw on any resources within to face temptation and to decide "to do the right thing." Personally, I would always prefer to replace the temptation with a new commitment to working things out in the marriage, and this ritual can be reworked with that focus. However, often it is made clear to me that what is needed most is strength. Based upon that, and a recurring unwillingness on the part of participants to hold this particular ritual in the sanctuary ("with the presence of God so close"), I decided to focus more on a ritual-type prayer, done in the pastor's office. The following is the result.

—◦◦◦—

Items Needed: Prepare for this ritual with a small nail, some anointing oil, and a Bible.

Pastor: Creator God, you who have made us and known us from our mother's womb, be present with us today as we come before you to ask for strength and the power of your Holy Spirit. _____ is facing a tremendous challenge in a time when personal resources seem almost gone. Come and sit with us, Lord, come and give us wisdom, Lord, not so much to discern your will, for that is clear, but to strengthen _____ to do your will when it is so very difficult, and when it seems so far from the desires of _____'s own heart.

Scripture Reading—*Choose from any of the Gospel accounts of Jesus' temptation in the wilderness.*

(Following the reading from scripture, invite the person to clearly define the task and how they might resist the temptation when it arises in the future. Some pastoral help might be needed during this exploration of alternatives.)

Pastor: I place in your hand this small nail to carry with you in the days to come. When your situation becomes difficult, hold this nail in your hand and remember that Jesus endured pain beyond imagining—for you. Remember that Jesus loved *you* enough to have nails driven through his body to hold him upon the cross on which he would die for you. Remember that you are not alone in your suffering, in your pain, or in your need for love.

Pastor: Let us pray. Loving Father, your child is searching to be fulfilled in this life by a loving relationship. The dream of a contented marriage is past, the present holds little hope, and the future is full of fear. Come and abide with us in the coming weeks. When the temptation to satisfy these deep longings becomes overwhelming, strengthen _____ with your eternal love. Give him/her a sense of your presence that is so real that these desires will pale in the warmth of your care for your own precious child. *(Anointing head or hands)* Touch this life, and empower it to confront the demons that seem ever near. Teach _____ daily about the path that you would walk together, and bring us all the abundant life that you have promised. We pray these things in the name of your beloved Son, Jesus, our Savior and our Lord. Amen.

Blessing Ritual for Letting Go of the Single Life

"Rejoicing in Companionship"

Comments: A young couple who had recently become engaged to be married were experiencing fear about giving up the lives they had individually established as single adults in the years following college. I suggested that we might begin their premarital counseling sessions with a brief ritual and asked them to bring an item to their next session which would symbolize their lives before and after their decision to wed. The ritual action was made more acute as they searched for and defined these symbols. If you want to provide examples to get them started, some of my favorites are a flower ("his love makes me blossom"), a framed picture ("she has brought me in line and into focus"), and even a popped kernel of popcorn ("this experience has been one that is full of pressure, but it has allowed me to come out of my shell"). The ritual was performed in my office, prior to their first counseling session.

Items Needed: *Prepare beforehand three candles and a Bible.*

Pastor: Let's begin in the name of the Father, who created you both; and of the Son, who loved you so much that he gave all that he had for you; and of the Holy Spirit, who dwells within each of you and will dwell within your life together. Amen.

_____ and _____ , you have come here this evening with symbols of your lives. These symbols represent both who you have been and who you are beginning to be, and we celebrate the change and the growth that you are about to experience because of the new stage of your lives, that stage that brings you together in a new reality, the reality of marriage. As you begin your sharing with me and with each other, please light one candle.

(Each one lights a candle and shares briefly about his or her symbol.)

Pastor: You have shared with each other an image of how your lives are changing as you move into this new phase. Let's offer ourselves and our session together to God in prayer: Gracious God, source of love and life, _____ and _____ have come before you poised for their new adventure and excited about what is to come. There is still a certain sadness which remains in their hearts as they say good-bye to many wonderful years of single life. Allow them to change and to grow together as their friendships shift and adapt to them as a couple. Keep them always connected to each other and to you with the goodness of honesty and the strength of your love, which is the source and ground of their love. Abide with them through the coming years and keep them always attentive to you and to each other as they share of themselves through the gift of their union. Amen.

To symbolize the union now beginning, light the third candle with both candles which the couple has lit. Do not blow out the couple's individual candles; for even though they will become one flesh, they will not relinquish their own flesh!

BLESSING RITUAL FOR LETTING GO OF LOST LOVE

"HOPE SPRINGS ETERNAL"

<u>Comments:</u> People sometimes have a hard time letting go of "old boyfriends/girlfriends." In many instances, there is little or no real contact with the previous love. Yet somehow the memories or the fantasies in connection with a past relationship continue to haunt the person. Often, there has been no intentional closure to the former relationship. Either the other party simply drifted away, there was a move and loss of contact, or there was never a satisfactory definition of the relationship in the first place. To address these "lost" loves, it is important to affirm the emotional attachment which was/is at the root of this relationship. The capacity to love deeply is truly a gift from God, and to relinquish any love is cause for sadness. This is especially true if there is currently no other relationship or relationships to replace it. This ritual is appropriate, with some adjustments for relationships that have passed, in situations where there is now a new relationship, or where the person remains solitary.

Items Needed: Preparation should include the person's choice of symbol and at least one large candle. During the ritual, an old science experiment is used—when you extinguish a flame, the smoke curls upward; if a lighted match is held in the smoke stream, the flame will "jump" down the smoke stream to relight the wick of the candle. You may wish to practice this maneuver so that the desired effect can be accomplished at the proper time in this ritual.

Pastor: We begin in the name of the Father, and of the Son, and of the Holy Spirit. Amen.

Heavenly Father, Creator of all things, you have shown us how to love by sacrificing your precious Son so that we might live. You surround us with your loving grace each day, and for this we give you thanks. We have gathered today to pray for peace in the heart of _____ , who grieves the loss of a special person in their past. *(You may name the person, if they were previously named openly.)*

When these two people were together, _____ experienced the joy that love brings to the human heart. Today, that joy has turned to sorrow, as your child grieves the loss of a loving relationship. We ask you, dear Creator, to send your Holy Spirit today to fill up the space that has been left by this loss. Encourage _____ and direct him/her in their journey in life, so that new loves may be found and that joy restored. *(Present the symbol that has been chosen to represent the person or the relationship which has been lost; you may wish to affirm the choice of symbol and suggest some other use or means of disposition.)*

(Lighting the candle) Creator God, as you called the light out of darkness, we ask you to bring light into the dark space in _____'s heart. Continue to strengthen him/her with the hope that you are the Light of the World and that with your light and your ministry to fill him/her, there is comfort to be found. *(Extinguish the candle and relight it as described above.)* Remind him/her that just as loving relationships come and go, the fire of your love stands always ready to rekindle the joy that love brings into our hearts. As _____ says a final farewell to his/her ended relationship with _____ , we give thanks for the love they shared and celebrate their parting as another marker on the journey. Bless each of them as they fully appreciate what they have today.

May the peace of God, which passes all our understanding, keep your heart and your mind in Christ Jesus. Amen. Go in peace to love and serve the Lord. Amen.

BLESSING RITUAL FOR LETTING GO OF PRIZED POSSESSIONS

"GO, SELL WHATEVER YOU HAVE AND GIVE TO THE POOR"

<u>Comments:</u> Difficulties sometimes arise surrounding the loss of a prized possession, whether it be due to the aftermath of a house fire, an estate sale, or a home or family farm being taken for highways. These losses are significant not for the possession itself but for the memories and emotions that are attached to it, sometimes for several generations. A seminary classmate recounted the story of the loss of her family's farm to a new highway. One year she returned home and, like Gertrude Stein's observation about Oakland, "there was no there there." She had left the home of her youth on her last visit, and returned to visit a different place, a house where her parents lived. In our mobile society, this kind of loss has become almost routine, and is often difficult to identify. The following ritual is designed to help people deal with the resulting emotions of such a loss.

Items Needed: *Preparation should include the choosing of an object to represent the lost item. Have two Bibles on hand.*

Pastor: Let us begin together by reading from the book of Ecclesiastes, chapter 3, verses 1-8. *(Read together.)*

_____ , you have come with a heavy heart over the loss of a place/thing/situation that you have loved. God has blessed you and your family with health and life itself, with warm and caring relationships, with work and play to feed your soul. Within this abundance there has been a significant loss, and we join here today to mark the grief that you have experienced at this loss.

Although you know that the loss of _____ is merely the passing of something transitory, the years of care and memories shared have brought deeper meaning to _____. It is the distancing from these memories and the loss of the existence of that place/item that is the source of your grief.

(The person may share the symbol and its meaning. Discuss together the meaning of the item itself, the disposition of the symbol in whatever appropriate fashion, and make a point to affirm the emotions surrounding the loss.)

Pastor: Let us pray. O God who has created all things and given us the beauty of this earth and of our relationships among your people, come and dwell with us today as we grieve the loss of _____. Send your Holy Spirit as a powerful reminder to *(name)* that the love shared and the memories experienced in connection with _____ will remain as long as he/she desires to recall them.

(At this point, you may actually dispose of the symbol. It may be destroyed by burning, purified by baptismal water, buried, thrown away, or given to an appropriate recipient.)

Bless _____ and impart your loving hope in the promise that even though heaven and earth will pass away, your love will never end. Strengthen the faith of all your children as we seek to remain steadfast in your care, doing your work in this world, until we are reunited with you and with those we love, in the kingdom that has no end.

We pray these things in the name of Jesus Christ, your Son, our Lord. Amen.

BLESSING RITUAL AROUND THERAPY FOR A DISEASE

"EMBRACING WHOLENESS"

Comments: A man was diagnosed with cancer in the fall. Although relatively healthy throughout most of his life, the diagnosis was a shock but not a surprise. His family history was rife with the disease, and as he shared with me, "It was only a matter of time." Having had intimate knowledge of the courses of treatment available and the effects of that treatment made this particular situation easier to discuss, but all of the emotions of the less knowledgeable were still evident. As we created this ritual, we talked at length about the burgeoning research data available regarding the positive attitude of cancer patients, and how prayer and hope were critical to the therapeutic process.

Items Needed: Prepare for this ritual with some type of planting items. Since this diagnosis came in the fall of the year, bulbs were readily available, and should be even throughout the winter in indoor varieties such as the paperwhite narcissus. In the spring and summer months, fast-growing seeds could be used. If indoors, have a pot, soil, trowel, and bulb/seed on hand, as well as a place prepared for the actual planting. If weather permits, you may wish to plant outside. Location may be the church's own garden or a site of the counselee's choice.

Pastor: We begin in the strong name of God our Creator, who planted for us a goodly garden in which to live, and still sustains us through the water of our Baptism and the nourishment of his Holy Supper.

_____ , you have come here to give your grieving

into God's care, and to ask for God's blessing as you begin the battle against the disease which has invaded your body.

Let us pray: O God, your precious child is calling on you today, and in faith and trust is asking for your presence in a powerful way in his life. We believe in your promise of abundant life, we thank you for the health that _____ has enjoyed for so many years, and we are confident that you will be with us as we begin a new journey together.

Take all of his anger and grief, his fear and his pain, and wrap them in your loving arms of health. Keep him secure in the love of his family and this community, and bring him courage and strength to face each day focused only on you.

As we plant this bulb/seed in the ground that you yourself created, we ask that you might use this growth as a symbol to _____ of the miracle of life and health. Allow him to ponder the cycle of growing on his journey: first the dark coolness of the surrounding earth, the stretching and reaching in that darkness for the source, you his light and his life. Let him feel the waters of Baptism bathing his whole body and soothing his pain, and nourish him often on your own body and blood, for the growth of his spirit and his very health. And, finally, bring him through the night and the darkness into the brilliance of your own light, that he might continue to grow and bring forth fruit among your faithful people in the world. *(The bulb/seed is planted.)*

Bless _____ as you bless the growth of this wondrous example of your creation. We pray in the name of the Great Physician, your Son, Jesus Christ, our Lord. Amen.

Blessing Ritual for Letting Go of Health

"Learning to Accept Another Gift"

Comments: A nervous disorder began to restrict a man's movement at about midlife. Having been an active member of the community for many years, the advancing stages of his illness took more of a toll on his self-esteem than on his physical body. For a person who had been in charge of family, business and self for so long, it was extremely difficult to allow others to help. Initially, family members spoke with me about how to deal with their loved one, who had become withdrawn and irritable, especially to those closest to him. This ritual is intended to help and support family caregivers. My hope was that in overhearing the family ritual, the patient might find some small ways to let go of his prideful responses and allow himself to accept the circumstances which his illness had brought upon him. With minor changes, this ritual could be adapted for use with a person suffering from a disabling disease or syndrome and the changes which ensue.

———

Items Needed: *Prepare the ritual space with a Bible, anointing oil, if desired, and a variety of symbols of the church year. For example, Advent candles, Christmas greens, Easter lilies, a cross, different-colored paraments, or other items that will be meaningful "time markers."*

Pastor: We have gathered together in the presence of God to ask for strength to accept life changes which are not of our choosing. We have been assured by Scripture that wherever two or more or gathered in Christ's name, there Christ will be, in the midst of them.

— 114 —

Let us pray. Heavenly Father, you who have called us forth to be workers in your vineyard, we come to you today to pray for _____ , who has had to adapt to the changes in his life and lifestyle because of the disease that has invaded his body. We know that changes are part of your created order, and we ask for the strength to accept whatever has occurred, always looking to you to be our steadfast hope in this life.

Scripture Reading—*Psalm 139, Ecclesiastes 3:1-8, the Beatitudes (Matt. 5), or other appropriate scripture, depending on individual circumstance.*

Pastor: Just as our community of faith celebrates each changing season of the church year, each of us must experience seasons and cycles in our own lives. _____ is now feeling the restrictions of a body that is changing every day. This gathering of family and friends who give care to _____ have come here to connect once again with the source of all life and health and to remember God's promise of new life and new creation in the fullness of God's kingdom.

If possible, connect this situation within the context of the church year, and highlight whatever symbol you have available. For example, the easiest would be the season of Lent, when Jesus himself was tempted for forty days in the wilderness immediately following his Baptism. Christmas and Easter are rife with possibilities to discuss birth and new life, salvation and resurrection. During the season of Pentecost, connection could be made to the growing season, where the church celebrates discipleship and spiritual development in the midst of everyday work in this world.

Pastor: Throughout his life on earth, Jesus himself depended on the care of many around him. He was nurtured by Mary, his mother; tended by women disciples; and accompanied by twelve good friends. Angels sustained him in the wilderness, and God gave him strength often as he removed himself to pray. Even at the end, when it seemed he was abandoned, a man named Joseph shared his own tomb for Jesus' burial. As we move through this life on earth, we are often dependent on others to support us and love us, to care for us and even to do for us. It is the ministry of God's love which gives us strength to both give of ourselves in this way and to receive that care with graciousness and humility.

Let us pray: *(You may anoint the sick and/or the caregivers.)* O God, we call upon you to strengthen the weak, and to support those who are your hands of love. Bless _____ and all who care for him in the coming days. Sustain his faith, renew his love, and give peace to his soul. We pray all these things in Jesus' name. Amen.

Close with the Lord's Prayer, spoken in unison.

BLESSING RITUAL FOR LETTING GO OF A PARENT'S ROLE

"ASSUMING NEW RESPONSIBILITIES"

Comments: Almost all parents face the time when their first child/children/last child leaves home and they become "empty nesters." For some, this time is one of release and newfound freedom. For others, it becomes a time of deep depression and loss, even fear at facing days on end without the loving chaos of a house full of family. Often parents have a difficult time adjusting to their last child's leaving home for college. The head agrees and understands, but the heart has not quite come to grips with the new arrangement. As I have mentioned before, the focus in any letting go should be on what is now possible rather than what is no longer possible.

Items Needed: Prepare by securing a "spiritual gifts inventory" of some sort. Allow approximately 30 minutes for the filling out of the inventory, tallying and affirming of gifts. If this type of instrument is not already in use in your parish or you do not have access to one of the various types readily available, review your own knowledge of the person prior to this ritual, so that you will be able to affirm those gifts which may not have been shared within your community, especially those that have remained untapped due to the responsibilities of parenting.

Pastor: We begin in the name of the Father, and of the Son, and of the Holy Spirit. Amen.

Let us pray: Creator God, author of our lives and giver of our gifts, we come to you most humbly this day to receive your blessing on this new phase of life for _____. As with any change, there is sadness at what has passed at the same time that there is celebration at the newfound freedom for his/her child, who has grown up with _____'s constant care and nurture and is now maturing in a new and exciting way. We pray for *(name the child)*, for your guidance and protection, for your love and continuing faith development, as he/she moves through this new portion of his/her journey with you.

Bless _____ through this transition and send the powerful presence of your Holy Spirit to direct these coming days ever closer to you. Amen.

_____, as we ponder what your life will focus upon in the coming months and years, it will be helpful for you to evaluate the gifts and talents with which God has so richly blessed you. One of the ways we can do this is for you to complete this inventory. Take your time, and then we will tally your responses and discuss it together. *(Take a break while the inventory is completed.)*

Upon completion of the inventory (or with your personal knowledge of the person), affirm those gifts and talents that can be utilized within the community. Suggest some ways that the emptiness might be filled through service to others. Emphasize not only the "doing for others" but finding a balance for much-needed solitude, perhaps starting small, with some devotional assignments, and increasing the joy of this time apart as the person adapts to this life change.

Pastor: God has richly blessed us with you in our midst! May you continue to serve our Lord in your life's ministry, seeking always to identify and be a good steward of all that you are, all that you have and all that you do. *(Lay on hands.)* I bless you for this new phase of your ministry, in the name of Jesus Christ, our Lord. Amen.

BLESSING RITUAL FOR BEING UNLOVED BY SOMEONE WHO SHOULD HAVE LOVED YOU

Comments: Often I have heard painful stories that have at their root the fact that someone who should have loved my parishioner did not. This is most often a parent who for whatever reason would not or could not share the affection so deeply sought after by his or her own child. Sometimes the story applies to a spouse or a child. If these people are still living and available for conversation, every effort should be made to counsel in the area of communication. However, if this is a story from long ago, and the people are no longer living, this type of ritual might be helpful. Note: Especially in the case of deceased parents, if you have knowledge of a professional counselor who works with the "re-parenting" techniques, refer the parishioner to that counselor.

—*∞*—

Items Needed: A Bible. Focus your scripture reading on God's mercy and forgiveness, whatever passage might be most meaningful for the particular situation.

Pastor: O most gracious heavenly Creator *(refrain from using "father" in this case if the issue is with the person's earthly father)*, we have come into your presence to ask for healing of an old hurt, and we humbly pray for your gentle touch of love upon this, your child.

In the waters of our Baptism we were given the gift of the presence of your Holy Spirit and were claimed by you as your beloved child. But, Lord, that gift of love was somehow absent in this family, and the grieving has imprinted this life for too many years.

Today we ask you to come in a powerful way into this life; replace the sadness and the pain of feeling unloved with the warmth and light of your eternal care. Allow this child to recall (*his or her parent/spouse/child*) through *your* heavenly eyes rather than his/her earthly ones, always mindful that although human and full of human frailties, their loved ones were nonetheless precious children of you as well. Teach us all your path of mercy, and give us strength to walk upon it.

Grant that forgiveness might fill this heart where pain has lived for so long. Bless _____ , your precious child, allow peace to replace the struggle and your precious love to soothe the hurt, so that in the end, the memory may be healed, and a new creation take its place.

We pray this in the confident hope that we can accomplish all things through you, our Creator and Redeemer, who gives us the strength and courage to do them. Amen.

BLESSING RITUAL AND NAMING OF A CHILD UNBORN/STILLBORN/THAT NEVER WAS

<u>Comments:</u> The many painful emotions which surround the memories of children who did not live have at their root unfulfilled hopes and dreams. A couple originally came in to review some marital difficulties. Through our discussions it became clear that the issue was not between them, but within the wife, who had suffered the loss of a child through stillbirth many years before. In conversation with her about the loss, it was revealed that even though the hospital had seemingly done all the right things, allowing her to hold the baby and spend time with it after the birth, there was some piece missing. She referred to the child throughout our counseling sessions as "the baby" and it occurred to me that she never even divulged the gender of the child. My first reaction was that "the baby" had not been baptized, and that there had been some regrets on that score, but on further exploration I was told that an emergency baptism had been done by the hospital chaplain. The only thing missing was that "the baby" had not been named.

The couple affirmed the fact that neither of them had ever referred to their child as anything other than "the baby." It was as if the impersonal reference could keep the hurt at a distance. The following ritual is really a prayer journey to "discover" the baby's name. It can be adapted for many purposes, and is useful in imagining the infant only dreamed of, never conceived, never birthed, or who did not survive to be named.

Items Needed: If possible, darken the room and light a candle. Soft meditative music may be played in the background, at a barely perceptible level. Speak slowly, allowing time for the images to come.

Pastor: We begin today by placing ourselves in the care of our God, the Father, the Son, and the Holy Spirit. Amen.

Close your eyes and concentrate on your breathing. Breathe in God's Spirit as you inhale, and breathe out your grief as you exhale. Imagine the ceiling is a star-filled sky; it is a warm summer night and the heavens are aglitter with cosmic light. You are in a place that has always been a haven for you, and you are feeling completely at peace.

In the sky far off you see one of the stars moving toward you, increasing its speed and size every moment, and you realize that whatever it is is coming directly overhead. You can begin to distinguish the shape. Can it be? Yes, it is an angel, and it has a small bundle in its arms. As it lights above you, the angel says softly, "Don't be afraid, hold this for a moment," and places in your arms a perfect child, a girl *(boy)*, a tiny, living infant. You look up at the angel with questioning eyes, and the angel replies again, ever so softly, "God wants you to name this child." You look into the tiny face, and the name that has always been there comes to your lips. You speak to the child, the name that has always been meant for her *(him)*. Say it now. Say it out loud.

(Leave time for her to speak the name; this may be very difficult, even overwhelming.)

The name is perfect, and as you raise your eyes to look at the angel, you realize you are once again alone. The night is as it was, the stars decorating the darkness, and you feel a wonderful sense of peace. And in the night sky far, far off in the distance you can see Jesus, with _____ in his arms.

(Wait for 15 to 30 seconds. Count them. If the person doesn't break the silence unassisted, speak softly, "Amen." Invite conversation, but don't force it. Close with a simple prayer of thanksgiving for the blessing of the life of _____.)

CHAPTER
FIVE

Creating Blessing Rituals

By now you probably have a pretty good grasp of how to create your own rituals and blessings. If you feel that you need a structure, please use the following outline:

1. Talk About the Ritual

Begin with conversation with those who will be involved in creating the ritual. Decide what is the most important effect that is desired. Is this a blessing to remind those involved that God is connected to this event? Is this a ritual which has as its end a transformation or new beginning? The answers to these questions will provide the framework for the ritual, and the final focus will depend on what your people need.

2. Make Necessary Decisions

Decide what setting is the most appropriate for the ritual or blessing. Is this a public event, or should it include only you and the person? Would they like to include others who played or will play a significant role in the event? How will these persons be contacted and invited, and do they need to be prepared with instructions beforehand?

3. Choose Appropriate Symbolism

Discuss how a physical symbol can play an important part in the service. Assist the person, if necessary, in the choice of symbol to be used within the service and the disposition of this symbol, if that is appropriate.

4. Don't Forget God

Make sure that you begin with an invocation and use texts from Scripture whenever possible. Finish each ritual by giving thanks to God.

5. Involve the Senses

Include earthly elements, especially if the participants do not bring their own symbols. Try to incorporate water, oil, fire, earth, incense, food, music, and so forth. Be aware of all the senses and attempt to create an atmosphere that will use all five: sight, smell, touch, taste, and sound.

6. Make Sacramental Connections

Whenever possible, recall the participants rootedness in Christ through their Baptism, which claimed them as God's precious children. Remember the ultimate sacrifice of love on their behalf by recalling the Lord's Supper or nourishing their lives by sharing Holy Communion.

7. Pray

Surround the entire ritual or blessing with prayer. Pray over them. Let them pray over you and for themselves. Do not let any opportunity to talk directly to God pass you by.

Once again, blessings on your leadership as you journey with your fellow travelers on the road of this life. And don't forget to write down your rituals and blessings. Once you start, you will not be able to stop . . . and even if you want to, your people probably won't let you. Such is the power of blessings and rituals. May the wisdom of Solomon and the patience of Job surround your efforts. And may the peace of God, which passes all understanding, keep your hearts and minds in Christ Jesus. Amen.

Notes

Chapter 1. Stepping Into . . . : Blessing Rituals for Children

1. Edward Hays, "Psalm During Pregnancy," in *Prayers for a Planetary Pilgrim* (Leavenworth, Kans.: Forest of Peace Publishing, 1989), p. 155.
2. Robert Fulghum, *From Beginning to End: The Rituals of Our Lives* (Villard/Random House, 1995), pp. 165-75.
3. *Lutheran Book of Worship* (Minneapolis: Augsburg Publishing House and Philadelphia: Board of Publication, Lutheran Church in America. 1978), p. 121.
4. Ibid.
5. Ibid.
6. Ibid.
7. Ibid.

Chapter 2. Marking the Journey: Blessing Rituals for Adults

1. *Lutheran Book of Worship* (Minneapolis: Augsburg Publishing House and Philadelphia: Board of Publication, Lutheran Church in America, 1978), p. 121.
2. Ibid.
3. Ibid, p. 201
4. Ibid, p. 203.

Chapter 3. Daily Living: Blessing Rituals for Everyday Life

1. Kathleen C. Szaj, *I Hate Goodbyes!* (Mahwah, N.J.: Paulist Press, 1997), p. 9.

Chapter 4. Letting Go: Blessing Rituals for Pastoral Care

1. Adapted from the *Lutheran Book of Worship* (Minneapolis: Augsburg Publishing House and Philadelphia: Board of Publication, Lutheran Church in America, 1978), p. 69.

BIBLIOGRAPHY

Artress, Lauren. *Walking a Sacred Path Rediscovering the Labyrinth as a Spiritual Tool.* New York: Riverhead Books, 1995.

de Mello, Anthony. *Wellsprings: A Book of Spiritual Exercises.* New York: Doubleday, 1984.

Driver, Tom F. *The Magic of Ritual: Our Need for Liberating Rites That Transform Our Lives and Our Communities.* San Francisco: Harper, 1991.

Fulghum, Robert. *From Beginning to End: The Rituals of Our Lives.* New York: Villard Books, 1995.

Hays, Edward. *Prayers for a Planetary Pilgrim.* Leavenworth, Kans.: Forest of Peace Publishing, 1989.

Kitchens, James A. *Talking to Ducks: Rediscovering the Joy and Meaning in Your Life.* New York: Fireside, 1994.

Lathrop, Gordon W. *Holy Things: A Liturgical Theology.* Minneapolis: Fortress Press, 1993.

Lutheran Book of Worship. Minneapolis: Augsburg Publishing House and Philadelphia: Board of Publication, Lutheran Church in America, 1978.

Nelson, Gertrud Mueller. *To Dance with God: Family Ritual and Community Celebration.* New York: Paulist Press, 1986.

Panati, Charles. *Sacred Origins of Profound Things.* Middlesex: Arcana, 1996.

Ramshaw, Elaine. *Ritual and Pastoral Care.* Philadelphia: Fortress Press, 1987.

Scotto, Dominic F. *The Liturgy of the Hours.* Petersham, Mass.: St. Bede's Publications, 1987.

Szaj, Kathleen C. *I Hate Goodbyes!* Mahwah, N.J.: Paulist Press, 1997.

Wright, Wendy M. *Sacred Dwelling: A Spirituality of Family Life.* New York: Crossroad Publishing Co., 1989.